GET READY TO WRITE

A Beginning Writing Text

SECOND EDITION

Karen Blanchard

Christine Root

PEARSON
Longman

This book is dedicated to our families, friends, colleagues, and students
for their help beyond all measuring.

Acknowledgments

We are grateful to Jeff Diluglio, John Dumicich, Carolyn Graham, Jane Sloan, and Robby Steinberg for helping us keep the purpose of this text in focus. We would also like to express our appreciation to our editor, Laura LeDréan, for her unfailing support and to Margot Gramer, Mike Kemper, Michael Mone, and Sarah Spader for their contributions to this second edition.

Reviewers

Leslie Bush-Corpuz, Tidewater Community College, Virginia Beach, VA; **Linda Butler**, Holyoke Community College, Holyoke, MA; **Terry Hirsch,** Waukegan High School, Waukegan, IL; **Barbara Smith-Palinkas**, University of South Florida, Tampa, FL; **Daina Smuidrins**, Shoreline Community College, Shoreline, WA; **Christine Ward**, Central Connecticut State University, New Britain, CT.

Get Ready to Write, Second Edition

Copyright © 2006, 1998 by Pearson Education, Inc.
All rights reserved.
No part of this publication may be reproduced, stored in a retrieval system, or transmitted in any form or by any means, electronic, mechanical, photocopying, recording, or otherwise, without the prior permission of the publisher.

Pearson Education, 10 Bank Street, White Plains, NY 10606

Staff credits: Laura LeDréan, Margot Gramer, Sarah Spader, Mike Kemper, Michael Mone, Melissa Leyva, Nancy Flaggman
Cover and text design: Pat Wosczyk
Text composition: Rainbow Graphics
Text font: 11.5/13 Goudy
Text art: Susan Detrich, Tom Sperling
Text credits: "Class Books of Robby Steinberg 1993-1996 (Haiku Poems)" by Vasakorn Bhadranavik, Kaya Karasawa and Fumihiko Suita. Reprinted with the permission of Roberta Steinberg. © 1996. "Memory Poem" from "Singing Chanting Telling Tales" by Carolyn Graham. Reprinted with the permission of Carolyn Graham.
Photo credits: Page 32, © Royalty-Free/Corbis; page 47, © 2003 Randy Glasbergen; page 68, © Muller/Gull/Getty Images; page 72, © Charles C. Ebbets/Bettmann/Corbis; page 76, © Sally A. Morgan; Ecoscene/Corbis; page 93, © Benjamin Rondel/Corbis; page 94, © Bettmann/Corbis; page 96, © Reuters/Corbis; page 98, © Bettmann/Corbis; page 100, © Hamilton/Associated Press; page 100, © Reuters/Corbis; page 113, © Randy Faris/Corbis

Library of Congress Cataloging-in-Publication Data

Blanchard, Karen Lourie, 1951–
  Get ready to write / Karen Blanchard, Christine Root.— 2nd ed.
    p. cm.
  ISBN 0-13-194635-8 (student book : alk. paper) — ISBN 0-13-198779-8 (answer key : alk. paper)
  1. English language—Textbooks for foreign speakers. 2. English language—Rhetoric—Problems, exercises, etc. 3. Report writing—Problems, exercises, etc. I. Root, Christine Baker, 1945– II. Title.
PE1128.B5865 2006
808'.042—dc22

2005025759

LONGMAN ON THE **WEB**

Longman.com offers online resources for teachers and students. Access our Companion Websites, our online catalog, and our local offices around the world.

Visit us at **longman.com**.

ISBN 0-13-194635-8

Printed in the United States of America
4 5 6 7 8 9 10–VHG–09 08 07 06

Contents

Introduction

Get Ready to Write is a beginning-level writing skills textbook for students of English as a Second Language who have some limited knowledge of both written and spoken English. *Get Ready to Write* is designed to acquaint students with the basic skills required for good writing and to help them become comfortable, confident, and independent writers in English.

APPROACH

Although it is a writing text, *Get Ready to Write* integrates reading, speaking, and listening skills with prewriting, planning, and rewriting. As in *Ready to Write* and *Ready to Write More*, students are called upon to write frequently and on a broad range of topics. *Get Ready to Write* is based on the premise that students at this level can and want to express themselves in English. What they need in order to do so effectively is an ever expanding vocabulary base and successive opportunities to write short, confidence-building pieces.

It is our intention in *Get Ready to Write* to introduce, without being overly didactic, the basic skills required for good writing in English. Through an abundance of pair and group activities as well as individual writing tasks, students learn the fundamental principles of prewriting, planning, drafting, revising, and editing as they move from sentence-level writing to guided paragraphs and beyond. We believe that having students write early and often instills in them the confidence necessary for successful writing.

THE SECOND EDITION

This second edition of *Get Ready to Write* features:

- additional model paragraphs
- guided practice in the stages of paragraph writing
- additional grammar practice
- sentence practice
- paragraph pointers
- real life writing activities
- appendices that include a reference on the English alphabet and penmanship; irregular verbs; and punctuation rules

Features popular in the previous edition have been expanded and continue to appear regularly in this new edition. "You Be the Editor" now focuses on the specific grammar point studied in each chapter. "Word Banks" have been enlarged to supply students with additional useful, pertinent vocabulary. "On Your Own" and "Use Your Imagination" provide students with further, less structured writing practice. Students are encouraged to assemble a "Portfolio" in a separate folder. This portfolio will be made up of the paragraphs, letters, poems, and drawings that students produce throughout the course.

We hope that you and your students enjoy the activities in this text as they *get ready to write*.

KLB and CBR

CHAPTER 1

Introducing Yourself

Getting Ready to Write

WRITING ABOUT YOURSELF

Learning to write in a new language is not always easy. It is hard, but it can also be fun. If you are learning to speak and read in a new language, you are ready to begin writing, too.

The easiest way to begin writing is to write about things you know well. That often means writing about yourself.

As you complete the exercises in *Get Ready to Write*, you will do a lot of writing about yourself and your life. You will find it interesting and helpful to keep your writing in a special folder called a *portfolio*.

MAKE A COVER FOR YOUR PORTFOLIO

A.   Look at the cover that a student designed for his portfolio.

B. Design the cover for your own portfolio on a separate piece of paper. Use drawings, pictures, and words to describe who you are. Here are some suggestions for things to include:

- Your family and friends
- Your interests and favorite activities
- Sports you like to play or watch
- Your job, profession, or major in school
- Your favorite places, foods, holidays, activities

C. Put your design on the cover of your portfolio.

D. Share the cover of your portfolio with your classmates.

- Show and explain the cover of your portfolio.
- Write your name on the chalkboard and teach your classmates how to pronounce it.
- Does your name have a special meaning in your language? What does it mean?
- Tell your classmates what language(s) you speak. Also tell them why you are studying English.

Word Bank

Arabic	German	Japanese	Rumanian
Cantonese	Greek	Korean	Russian
Czech	Hebrew	Mandarin	Spanish
Dutch	Indonesian	Polish	Thai
French	Italian	Portuguese	Vietnamese

Develop Your Writing Skills

WHAT IS A SENTENCE?

An English sentence always has a subject and a verb. Many sentences have an object, too. The most common order for English sentences is subject + verb + object.

The subject is a noun or pronoun. It is usually a person or thing that is doing the action. The verb tells the action. The object is also a noun or pronoun. It usually answers the question "what or who(m)."

Example

   Anna   speaks Russian.
(subject) (verb) (object)

   Paulo   plays soccer.
(subject) (verb) (object)

Most verbs, like *play*, *read*, *give*, *speak*, describe an action. A few other verbs called linking verbs are not action verbs. The most common linking verb is *be*. Sentences with linking verbs are followed by adjectives or nouns. These adjectives and nouns always tell us something about the subject of a sentence. They are called complements.

Example

    Anna   is   happy.
(subject) (linking verb) (complement)

    Paulo   is   a teacher.
(subject) (linking verb) (complement)

Circle the verb in each sentence. Underline the subject. Draw a box around the object or complement.

Example

Mr. Robertson (is) [tired.]

1. Chris kicked the soccer ball.

2. She is shy.

3. Andrea and Marshall ride bikes.

4. He is a banker.

5. We watch movies.

6. They are funny.

PREWRITING

A. Answer these questions about yourself in complete sentences.

1. What is your name?

    _____

2. Where are you from?

    _____

3. What language do you speak?

    _____

4. What do you do? (For example, are you a student? Are you a businessperson? Are you a secretary?)

    _____

5. What do you like to do? (For example, do you like to go to the movies? Do you like to read magazines? Do you like to listen to music? Do you like to go shopping?)

    _____

CAPITAL LETTERS

The first word of every sentence begins with a capital letter. Other important words in English begin with a capital letter, too. Follow these rules for using capital letters.

Rules	Examples
1. The first word of a sentence or question	What is his name? His name is Matthew Simmons.
2. The pronoun *I*	Harris and I like to play tennis together.
3. The names and titles of people	He has an appointment with Dr. Carol Wolf. Let's call Song Yee.
4. The names of countries, cities, states, continents, and streets	They live in Lima, Peru. Peru is in South America. She is from Austin, Texas The library is on Juniper Street
5. Days of the week and months of the year	His birthday is next Thursday. We're going on vacation in June.
6. The names of languages and nationalities	He speaks Vietnamese. My grandparents are Mexican.

Rewrite each sentence. Add the capital letters.

1. i like to travel.

   _____

2. yumi lives in tokyo, japan.

   _____

3. when did they get back from mexico?

   _____

4. mr. kim has a meeting on friday.

   _____

5. ali is studying spanish and english this semester.

   _____

6. my birthday is in july.

   _____

7. what do you want to do on sunday?

   _____

WHAT IS A PARAGRAPH?

Most English writing is organized into paragraphs. You will write many paragraphs in this book. A paragraph is a group of sentences about one main idea. This main idea is called the *topic*.

An English paragraph has a special form. Read the paragraph below. It is written in the correct form.

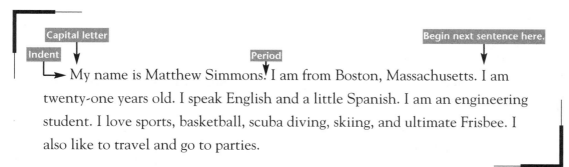

Capital letter

Indent

Period

Begin next sentence here.

My name is Matthew Simmons. I am from Boston, Massachusetts. I am twenty-one years old. I speak English and a little Spanish. I am an engineering student. I love sports, basketball, scuba diving, skiing, and ultimate Frisbee. I also like to travel and go to parties.

Paragraph Pointer: The Paragraph Form
1. Indent the first line of each new paragraph about two centimeters from the margin.
2. Begin each sentence with a capital letter.
3. End each sentence with a period.
4. Do not start each new sentence on a new line.

A. Look at the paragraph below. Talk about what is wrong with the form with a partner.

my name is Lilly Lang

I am 28 years old

I am from Atlanta, Georgia

my native language is English

I am an artist.

B. Write the paragraph in the correct form.

_____

_____

_____

_____

_____

WRITING

Use the sentences you wrote about yourself on page 3 to write a paragraph about yourself on the lines below. Be sure to follow the rules of paragraph writing.

My name is _____

_____

_____

_____

_____

REVISING

A. Exchange paragraphs with a partner. Read your partner's paragraph and check *yes* or *no* for each question on the Paragraph Checklist. Then help your partner improve his/her paragraph.

Paragraph Checklist		
	YES	NO
1. Is the first word of the paragraph indented?	❏	❏
2. Does each sentence begin with a capital letter?	❏	❏
3. Does each sentence end with a period?	❏	❏
4. Does each new sentence begin next to the one before it?	❏	❏

B. Use your partner's suggestions to revise your paragraph. Copy it onto a separate piece of paper. Give it the title "About Me" and put it in your portfolio.

PREWRITING

A. Talk to a classmate. Ask him/her these questions. Write the answers on the lines.

1. What is your name?

   _____

2. Are you married or single?

   _____

3. Where are you from?

   _____

4. What is your native language?

   _____

5. What do you do? (Are you a student? Are you a businessperson? Are you a secretary, a lawyer, or a musician?)

   _____

6. What do you like to do?

   _____

7. What else do you like to do?

   _____

B. Use the answers to complete the sentences about your classmate. Then copy the complete sentence on the line.

Example   My classmate's name is _Oscar_ .

   My classmate's name is Oscar.

1. My classmate's name is _____.

   _____

2. He/She is _____.

   _____

3. He/She is from _____.

   _____

4. He/She speaks _____.

_____

5. He/She is a _____.

_____

6. He/She likes to _____.

_____

7. He/She also likes to _____.

_____

WRITING

Use your sentences to write a paragraph about your classmate. Remember to follow the rules of paragraph writing.

My classmate's name is _____. _____

_____

_____

_____

_____

REVISING

A. Exchange paragraphs with your partner. Read the paragraph your partner wrote about you. Make sure the information about you is correct. Then use the Paragraph Checklist to help your partner improve his/her paragraph.

Paragraph Checklist		
	YES	**NO**
1. Is the first word of the paragraph indented?	❑	❑
2. Does each sentence begin with a capital letter?	❑	❑
3. Does each sentence end with a period?	❑	❑
4. Does each new sentence begin next to the one before it?	❑	❑
5. Are all of the sentences about you correct?	❑	❑

B. Use your partner's suggestions to revise your paragraph. Copy it onto a separate piece of paper and give it the title "My Classmate." Share your paragraph with your classmates. Put it in your portfolio.

On Your Own

Write a paragraph about your teacher or another one of your classmates. Use the Prewriting questions on page 7 to help you get started. Show your paragraph to a partner and use the Paragraph Checklist to improve your paragraph.

You Be the Editor

The paragraph *A Lucky and Happy Man* has eight mistakes in the use of capital letters. With a partner, find the mistakes and correct them.

A Lucky and Happy Man

My name is Stanley stoico. I am 90 years old. I am from italy. I moved to San Diego, california, with my family when I was nine years old. I speak italian and english. in my younger years, I had many different jobs. I worked hard and saved my money. In 1955, I started my own business. the business was successful, and i retired in 1983. I like to travel and play golf. I have seen and done a lot in my long life. I am a lucky and happy man.

Real Life Writing

FILLING OUT A FORM

Fill out the form below with information about yourself.

Student Information Form

Please print.

1. Name:_____

          Last   First   Middle

2. Address: _____

    _____

3. Phone Number: _____ E-mail: _____

4. Sex: _____ M _____ F

5. Marital Status: _____ Single _____ Married _____ Divorced _____ Widowed

6. Nationality:_____

7. First Language: _____

8. Other Languages: _____

9. How long have you studied English? (*Please check one.*)

    _____ Never

    _____ Less than 1 year

    _____ 1–2 years

    _____ More than 2 years

10. Do you work? _____ Yes _____ No

11. If yes, where? _____ What hours?_____

12. Signature: _____

CHAPTER 2

Writing about Your Family and Friends

Getting Ready to Write

WRITING ABOUT FAMILY

A. Look at Tom Brower's family tree. Then ask and answer the questions with a partner. Use the words in the Word Bank on the next page to help you.

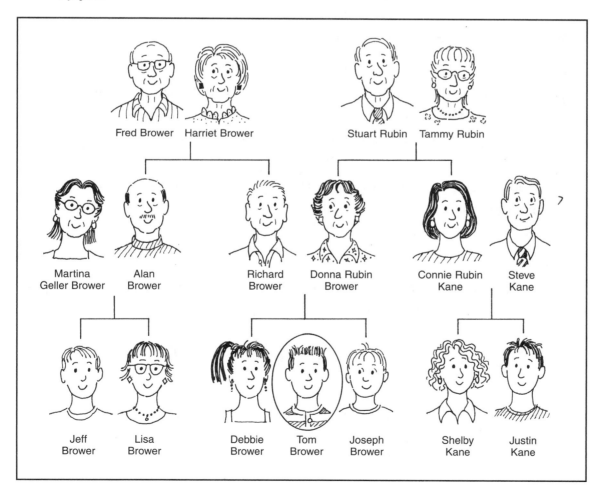

Fred Brower   Harriet Brower   Stuart Rubin   Tammy Rubin

Martina Geller Brower   Alan Brower   Richard Brower   Donna Rubin Brower   Connie Rubin Kane   Steve Kane

Jeff Brower   Lisa Brower   Debbie Brower   Tom Brower   Joseph Brower   Shelby Kane   Justin Kane

1. Who is Tom's mother? _____

2. Who is Tom's father? _____

3. What is Tom's sister's name? _____

4. What is Tom's brother's name? _____

5. How many cousins does Tom have? _____

6. Who are Tom's grandmothers? _____

Word Bank

aunt	grandaughter	married	son
brother	grandfather	mother	stepfather
child/children	grandmother	nephew	stepsister
cousin	grandson	niece	uncle
daughter	great grandfather	parents	wife
divorced	great grandmother	single	
father	husband	sister	

B. Read the paragraph Tom wrote about his family.

I have a big family, and we all get along very well. My parents' names are Richard and Donna Brower. I have one younger brother. His name is Joseph. He is 10 years old. I also have an older sister. Her name is Debbie. She is 19 years old. I have four cousins. Their names are Jeff Brower, Lisa Brower, Shelby Kane, and Justin Kane. I usually go out with them on the weekends. My grandparents love to invite us to their house for dinner. Whenever my family gets together, we have a great time.

C. On a separate piece of paper, draw your own family tree. Give it the title "My Family Tree" and put it in your portfolio.

Develop Your Writing Skills

SUBJECT AND OBJECT PRONOUNS

Pronouns are used to refer to a noun that has already been mentioned. Pronouns help you connect sentences without repeating the same nouns. Pronouns can be singular or plural. Two of the most common kinds of pronouns are subject pronouns and object pronouns.

Subject pronouns

Subject pronouns (such as *we, she, they*) serve as the subject of a sentence.

Examples

Debbie is my sister. **She** is 18 years old. (She = Debbie)
          (subject)

Abdullah is my cousin. **He** works at a bank. (He = Abdullah)
          (subject)

Singular (one person/thing)	Plural (two or more people/things)
I	we
you	you
he, she, it	they

A.   Underline the subject pronouns in the paragraph about Tom's family on page 12.

B.   Complete the second sentence in each pair with a pronoun.

1. Mrs. Petty is a teacher. _____ teaches English.

2. My car is green. _____ is new.

3. John and I are brothers. _____ are both students.

4. Steve and Chuck are cousins. _____ live in Taiwan.

5. Jorge loves sports. _____ plays basketball, soccer, and golf.

Object pronouns

Object pronouns serve as the object of a verb.

Examples

Fran called *Mrs. Davis.* Fran called **her.** (her = Mrs. Davis)
          (object)

David e-mailed *Stan* and *Joey.* David e-mailed **them.** (them = Stan and Joey)
          (object)

Singular	Plural
me	us
you	you
him, her, it	them

C. Circle the object pronouns in the paragraph about Tom's family on page 12.

D. Complete the second sentence in each pair with an object pronoun.

1. We called <u>Mr. Smith</u>. We called _____.

2. I drove <u>my mother</u> to the station. I drove _____ to the station.

3. Pam misses <u>her little boy</u>. Pam misses _____.

4. We e-mailed <u>our friends</u> last week. We e-mailed _____ last week.

POSSESSIVE ADJECTIVES

Possessive adjectives modify nouns to show ownership.

Examples

My sisters are very close.

Drew is selling **his** car.

The Ortegas painted **their** apartment.

Donna smiled at **her** mother.

Singular	Plural
my	our
your	your
his, her, its	their

A. Draw a box around the possessive adjectives in the paragraph about Tom's family on page 12.

B. Complete each sentence with the correct possessive adjective.

1. I like to spend time with _____ brothers.

2. My sister loves _____ new puppy.

3. My parents love _____ children.

4. Daniel likes to play games on _____ computer.

5. Suzanne and Gary enjoy playing with _____ cousins.

C. Complete the paragraph with the correct pronoun or possessive adjective.

    I love to look at _____*my*_____ (me, my) grandparents' old
            1.
photograph album. It is always fun to see pictures of _____
                                                                         2.
(me, my) mother when _____ (she, her) was a little girl.
                                      3.
_____ (She, Her) looks so cute with _____
     4.   5.
(she, her) curly hair and big smile. I also like looking at all of the different cars
my grandfather bought over the years. _____ (He, Him) loved
                                                           6.
_____ (him, his) cars, and he took very good care of
     7.
_____ (they, them). My favorite pictures are the ones of
     8.
_____ (me, my) parents' wedding. My mother and father look
     9.

nervous, but I am sure _____ (them, they) were very happy. The

10.

last part of the album is filled with pictures of _____ (my, me)

11.

and _____ (my, me) baby brother. I think I look like my mother

12.

when she was _____ (my, me) age. I am so glad my grandparents

13.

made this album.

PREWRITING

A. Answer these questions about your family.

1. How many people are there in your family? _____

2. What are your parents' names? _____
   Where do they live? _____

3. What does your father do? _____
   What does your mother do? _____

4. How many brothers and sisters do you have? _____ What are their names?
   _____ How old are they? _____

5. Do you have any children? _____ How many? _____ What are their
   names? _____ How old are they? _____

B. Write at least five sentences about your family.

1. _____

2. _____

3. _____

4. _____

5. _____

WRITING

Use your sentences to write a paragraph about your family. Begin by choosing an
adjective to complete the first sentence. Remember to follow the rules of paragraph
writing. Use at least five pronouns in your paragraph.

I have a _____ family . _____

(big/small/happy)

_____

_____

_____

_____

_____

REVISING

A. Exchange paragraphs with a partner. Read your partner's paragraph and check *yes* or *no* for each question on the Paragraph Checklist. Then help your partner improve his/her paragraph.

Paragraph Checklist		
	YES	**NO**
1. Is the first word of the paragraph indented?	❏	❏
2. Does each sentence begin with a capital letter and end with a period?	❏	❏
3. Does each new sentence begin next to the one before it?	❏	❏
4. Are there at least five pronouns?	❏	❏

B. Use your partner's suggestions to revise your own paragraph. Copy your paragraph onto a separate piece of paper. Give it the title "My Family" and put it in your portfolio.

PREWRITING

A. Think about someone in your family you would like to write about.

Write his/her name here. _____

B. Answer the questions about him/her.

1. How is this person related to you (a cousin/sister/brother)? _____

2. How old is he/she? _____

3. Is he/she married or single? _____

4. Where does he/she live? _____

5. What does he/she do? _____

6. What does he/she like to do? _____

C. Add one or two more interesting things about him/her.

_____

_____

WRITING

Use your sentences to write a paragraph about someone in your family. Use at least five pronouns in your paragraph.

My _____'s name is _____. _____

_____

_____

_____

_____

REVISING

A. Exchange paragraphs with a partner. Read your partner's paragraph and check *yes* or *no* for each question on the Paragraph Checklist. Then help your partner improve his/her paragraph.

Paragraph Checklist		
	YES	**NO**
1. Is the first word of the paragraph indented?	❑	❑
2. Does each sentence begin with a capital letter and end with a period?	❑	❑
3. Does each new sentence begin next to the one before it?	❑	❑
4. Are there at least five pronouns?	❑	❑

B. Use your partner's suggestions to revise your paragraph. Then copy it onto a separate piece of paper. Give it the title "My _____" (Example: My Brother) and put it in your portfolio.

USING *AND*, *BUT*, OR *SO*

When you write in English you can combine sentences using the words *and*, *but*, and *so* to make your writing more interesting. These words are called conjunctions.

Conjunction	Use	Example
and	joins two similar ideas together	Tom Brower has a close family, *and* he loves them very much.
but	joins two contrasting ideas	He enjoys spending time with them, *but* he doesn't get to see them very much.
so	shows that the second idea is the result of the first	Tom misses his family, *so* he keeps a photograph of the whole family on his desk.

A. Combine the pairs of sentences using *and*, *but*, or *so*.

1. Sandra goes out with her cousins. She goes out with her friends, too.

   _____

2. Maria would like to spend more time with her sisters. She is usually too busy.

   _____

3. Erin wants to e-mail her mother. Her computer is broken.

   _____

4. Min misses her brother. She calls him almost every day.

   _____

5. Ana doesn't have enough money to buy a new computer. She got a part-time job.

   _____

B. Compare your sentences with a partner's. Did you use the same words to combine the sentences?

C. Read the paragraph below and circle the conjunctions.

I have a good friend, José, and he is like a brother to me. He is very responsible, but he is also fun to be with. We have a great time whenever we get together. He is smart and reads a lot, so he always has interesting things to say. He is quite a talkative guy, but he is a very good listener, too. I can talk about my problems with him, and he always gives me good advice. I am really glad to have a friend like José.

Paragraph Pointer: The Writing Process

Writing a paragraph is a process that includes several steps. The steps in the process are called prewriting, writing, and revising. When you follow the steps, it will be easier to write a good paragraph.

Step One: Prewriting

Before you write a paragraph, it is helpful to think, talk, and make lists of ideas about the topic. This gets you ready to write.

Step Two: Writing

Use your prewriting ideas to help you write your paragraph.

Step Three: Revising

Make corrections and changes in your paragraph.

PREWRITING

A. In small groups, discuss the qualities of a good friend. Put a check next to the qualities that you think are important.

1. _____ responsible   5. _____ good listener   9. _____ loyal

2. _____ fun to be with   6. _____ honest   10. _____ warm

3. _____ kind   7. _____ good-looking

4. _____ intelligent   8. _____ wealthy

B. Choose a friend that you would like to write about and describe your friend to the people in your group.

Write his/her name here. _____

C. Fill in the following information about your friend.

1. How old is your friend? _____

2. Is your friend married or single? _____

3. Where does he/she live? _____

4. What does he/she do? _____

5. What does he/she like to do? _____

6. What adjectives would you use to describe your friend? _____

D. Add one or two more interesting facts about your friend.

_____

_____

WRITING

Use some of your sentences to write a paragraph about your friend. Remember to follow the rules of paragraph writing. Use at least five pronouns in your paragraph.

My friend's name is _____ . _____

_____

_____

_____

_____

REVISING

A. Exchange paragraphs with a partner. Read your partner's paragraph and check *yes* or *no* for each question on the Paragraph Checklist below. Then help your partner improve his/her paragraph.

Paragraph Checklist		
	YES	**NO**
1. Is the first word of the paragraph indented?	❏	❏
2. Does each sentence begin with a capital letter and end with a period?	❏	❏
3. Does each new sentence begin next to the one before it?	❏	❏
4. Are there at least five pronouns?	❏	❏

B. Use your partner's suggestions to revise your paragraph. Copy it onto a separate piece of paper. Put it in your portfolio with the title "My Friend _____."

On Your Own

Write a paragraph about another friend or a family member. Use the questions on page 20 to help you get started. Show your paragraph to a partner and use the Paragraph Checklist to improve your paragraph.

Use Your Imagination

A. Pretend it is the year 2025. Make a list of sentences about your family.

Example

I have a son named Stephen. He is getting married next week.

My daughter's name is Diana. She is the mayor of my hometown.

1. _____
2. _____
3. _____
4. _____
5. _____

B. Choose an adjective such as *wonderful, small, large, or unusual* to describe your "future" family and complete the first sentence. Then use your sentences to write a paragraph.

I have a _____ family. _____

_____

_____

_____

_____

_____

You Be the Editor

The paragraph *My Cousin* has five mistakes in the use of pronouns. With a partner, find the mistakes and correct them.

My Cousin

My cousin's name is Bettina Lee. She is 37 years old. She was born in Chicago, Illinois, but now her lives in Denver, Colorado. She is married and has two children. Bettina and me enjoy spending time together. Us love to go ice-skating. Bettina is an excellent ice-skater. She skated in ice shows when he was young. Now Bettina teaches ice-skating to young children. She enjoys watching their.

Real Life Writing

AN E-MAIL MESSAGE

Writing e-mail messages is a quick and easy way to communicate. E-mails are usually short and specific.

A. Read the sample e-mail below.

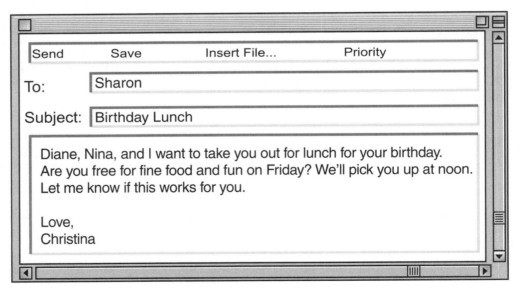

Send   Save   Insert File...   Priority

To: Sharon

Subject: Birthday Lunch

Diane, Nina, and I want to take you out for lunch for your birthday.
Are you free for fine food and fun on Friday? We'll pick you up at noon.
Let me know if this works for you.

Love,
Christina

B. Write an e-mail for each of the following situations.

1. Write an e-mail to your roommate, Juanita. Remind her to stop at the pizza shop on her way home and get a large mushroom pizza.

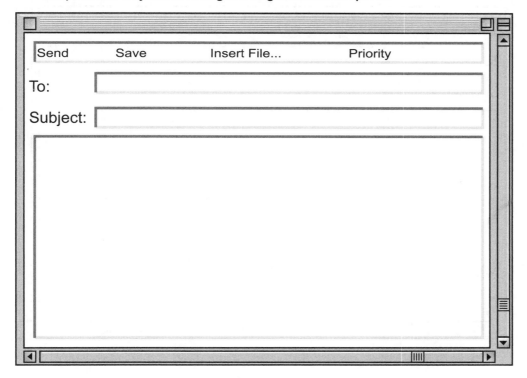

2. Write an e-mail to your friend Paul. Tell him that you are sorry, but you will not be able to meet him for dinner tonight. Ask him if tomorrow night is good for him.

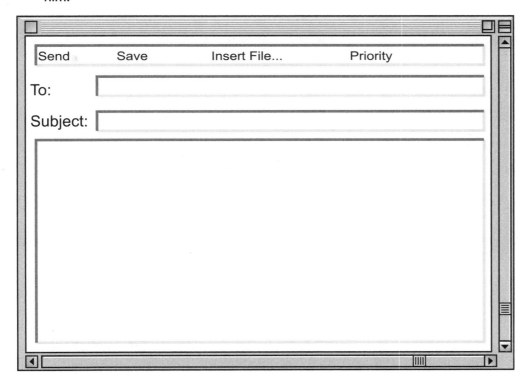

3. Write an e-mail to your co-worker. Tell him your car broke down. Ask him to give you a ride to work tomorrow morning.

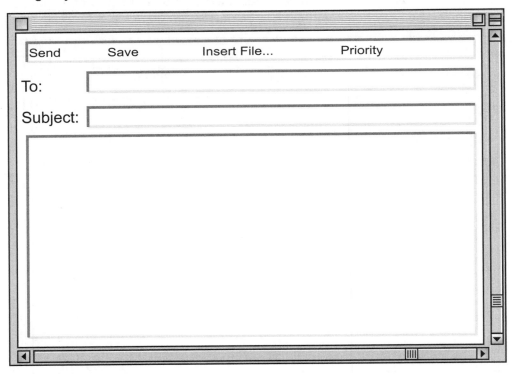

Send   Save   Insert File...   Priority

To:

Subject:

CHAPTER 3

Writing about Your Activities

Getting Ready to Write

WRITING ABOUT ACTIVITIES YOU LIKE

A.   Look at the five pictures below. They show the things a student named Eric likes to do with his friends. Write the name of the activity under the correct picture. Use the words in the Word Bank.

Word Bank

buying CDs	listening to music	playing soccer
going to the movies	playing computer games	

1. _____   2. _____   3. _____

4. _____   5. _____

B. Complete the paragraph below with words from the Word Bank on page 25. Be sure to use the correct form of the verb.

Spending Time with Friends

When he has free time, Eric enjoys spending time with his friends. They

often _____ soccer together after class. They also like
                        1.

playing computer _____ and going to the
                              2.

_____ together. Eric and his friends like
               3.

_____ to music, so they often go to the music store to
               4.

_____ new CDs. Sometimes they don't go anywhere,
               5.

but they aren't bored. They just sit around and talk and laugh. Eric and his

friends always have fun when they are together.

C. Talk to a partner. Ask and answer these questions.

1. What does Eric like to do in his free time?

2. What sport does Eric and his friends like to play?

3. What else does Eric like to do with his friends?

Develop Your Writing Skills

THE SIMPLE PRESENT TENSE

Verbs in the simple present tense have two forms: the *s* form and the base form. The form of the verb that you use depends on the subject of the sentence.

1. The *s* Form: When the subject is a singular noun (Cathy, the car, the dog, etc.) or a singular pronoun (he, she, or it), add *s* (or *es* or *ies*) to the verb.

2. The Base Form: When the subject is a plural noun (Cathy and Tom, the cars, the dogs, etc.), or one of the other pronouns (I, you, we, they), use the base form of the verb. Do not add *s*.

Examples

Eric **enjoys** spending time with his friends. He **likes** to play computer games with them.

I **enjoy** spending time with my friends. I **like** to go shopping with them.

Spelling Rules for Forming the *s* Form of the Simple Present Tense	Examples
1. For most verbs, add *s*	work—works play—plays
2. For verbs ending in consonant + *y*, change the *y* to *i* and add *es*	worry—worries
3. For verbs ending in *s, z, ch, sh, x*, add *es*	catch—catches
4. Irregular verbs	go—goes do—does have—has

The verb *be* has its own form in the present tense:

I *am* | he
she $\Big\}$ *is*
it | they
you $\Big\}$ *are*
we

A. The sentences below have mistakes in the use of the simple present tense verbs. Correct the mistakes.

1. Maria worrys about her children. _____

2. We plays soccer on the weekend. _____

3. You is never on time. _____

4. She wash her clothes at the laundromat. _____

5. Both of my sisters lives in Texas. _____

6. I has lots of new friends in my class. _____

7. I think he watchs too much TV. _____

B. Rewrite the paragraph. Change *I* to *Shelly* in the first sentence. Make all the necessary changes.

A Tired New Mother

I am a proud but tired mother of twin baby boys. I am very happy, but I am also tired all the time. I never get much sleep anymore. I wake up in the middle of the night and feed the babies. Then I change diapers all day long. I also wash baby clothes and blankets every morning and evening. Sometimes when both babies are crying at the same time, I cry, too. But when I watch them sleeping peacefully, I know how lucky I am to have two happy, healthy babies.

Shelly is _____ . _____

_____

_____

_____

_____

_____

PARTS OF A PARAGRAPH IN ENGLISH

Paragraph Pointer: Parts of a Paragraph
Most paragraphs have three main parts: 1. A topic sentence   2. Several supporting sentences   3. A concluding sentence

1. The _topic sentence_ is the most important sentence in the paragraph. It is often, but not always, the first sentence in the paragraph. The topic sentence tells the reader what the paragraph is about.

2. Next come the _supporting sentences_. These sentences give details, examples, and reasons to explain the topic sentence. All of the supporting sentences must relate to the topic of the paragraph.

3. Some paragraphs end with a _concluding sentence_. The concluding sentence restates the main idea in different words. Here are some common ways to begin a concluding sentence:

   > All in all,
   > As you can see,
   > In conclusion,

Work with a partner. Read each paragraph and identify the parts. Ask and answer the questions that follow.

1.   Serita likes to spend her free time outdoors. Her favorite outdoor activity is gardening, and she loves to plant new kinds of flowers in her garden every year. She also enjoys taking long walks in the park. On sunny days, Serita goes to the beach with her friends. As you can see, Serita loves being outside in her free time.

   a. What is the topic sentence?
   b. How many supporting sentences are there?
   c. What is the concluding sentence?

2.   I have several hobbies that keep me busy in my free time. I love to read, and I often read short stories and magazines. Another one of my hobbies is cooking, and Chinese cooking is my specialty. My favorite hobby is photography. I usually take black and white pictures because I think they are more interesting. In conclusion, without my hobbies, my life would not be as much fun.

    a. What is the topic sentence?
    b. How many supporting sentences are there?
    c. What is the concluding sentence?

USING *WHEN*

You can use *when* to show that two things happen at the same time.

Examples

Eric and his friends always have fun **when** they are together.

When they are together, Eric and his friends always have fun.*

*Note that we use a comma in sentences that start with *when*.

A. Combine the pairs of sentences using *when*. Use a comma.

1. I'm bored. I call my friends.

_____

2. My friends come over. We play video games.

_____

3. I don't exercise. I feel very tired.

_____

4. I go running. I have a lot of energy.

_____

B. Complete the sentences below. Then compare your sentences with a partner.

1. When I wake up in the morning, I _____.

2. When I get to school (work), I _____.

3. When I feel tired, I _____.

4. When I exercise, I _____.

PREWRITING

A. What do you like to do in your free time? Talk to a partner. Discuss some things that you like to do with your friends or family. Use the Word Bank to help you with vocabulary.

Word Bank

bake	go to museums	play guitar/piano	spend time online
cook	go to parties	play soccer	swim
dance	go to the movies	play tennis	take pictures
draw	listen to music	read	take walks
exercise/work out	paint	sew	talk on the phone
go shopping	play computer/video games	sing	travel
go to concerts	play golf	ski	watch TV

B. Make a list of the things you like to do.

_____   _____
_____   _____
_____   _____
_____   _____

C. Share your list with your partner. Talk about the things you like to do the most. Do you and your partner like to do any of the same things? Which ones?

D. Use your list to complete each of the following sentences.

1. I like to _____.

2. I also like to _____.

3. Another thing I enjoy is _____.

4. I like to _____, and I _____.

5. I enjoy _____, but I _____.

WRITING

Use your sentences to write a paragraph. Complete the topic sentence. Include at least four supporting sentences. Complete the concluding sentence.

When I have free time, I _____

_____

_____

_____

As you can see, _____

REVISING

A. Exchange paragraphs with a partner. Read your partner's paragraph and check *yes* or *no* to each question on the Paragraph Checklist. Then help your partner improve his/her paragraph.

Paragraph Checklist		
	YES	**NO**
1. Does each sentence begin with a capital letter and end with a period?	❏	❏
2. Does each new sentence begin next to the one before it?	❏	❏
3. Is there a topic sentence?	❏	❏
4. Are there at least four supporting sentences?	❏	❏
5. Is there a concluding sentence?	❏	❏

B. Use your partner's suggestions to revise your paragraph. Write your paragraph on a separate piece of paper and put it in your portfolio with the title "My Free Time."

WRITING ABOUT KEEPING FIT

A. Lots of people like to exercise to stay healthy. Look at the pictures of people exercising. Complete the sentences. Use the words in the word bank.

Word Bank

aerobic dancing	karate	swimming
bike	lifts weights	walking
cross-country skiing	running	yoga

1. Jason gets a lot of exercise when he goes _____.

2. Marsha _____ three times a week.

3. Jim goes _____ every morning before work.

4. Mark rides his _____ to school for exercise.

5. Alice takes _____ classes at her gym.

6. _____ is David's favorite kind of exercise.

7. Mr. Wolf goes _____ before dinner to exercise.

8. Hannah does _____ to relax.

9. Ian practices _____ once a week.

B. Study the vocabulary in the Word Bank. Then read the paragraph *Keeping Fit* and answer the questions.

Word Bank

exercise	keep fit	track
gym	stay healthy	work out
health club	stay in shape	

Keeping Fit

Steve Fredericks cares about keeping fit. First of all, he tries to get some exercise every day. He belongs to a health club where he usually exercises after work. He likes to lift weights and run on the track. In addition, he is careful about his diet. For example, he rarely eats foods that have a lot of fat or sugar. Finally, Steve tries to get eight hours of sleep every night. Like many of his friends, Steve tries to keep in shape and stay healthy.

1. What is the topic sentence? _____

2. What are three things that Steve does to support the fact that he cares about keeping fit?

   _____

   _____

   _____

3. What is the concluding sentence?

   _____

PREWRITING

A. Answer each question in a complete sentence. Then discuss your answers with a partner.

1. What kind of exercise do you enjoy?

   _____

2. How often do you exercise?

   _____

3. Do you eat healthy meals?

   _____

4. Do you smoke? If so, how much and when do you smoke?

   _____

5. Do you usually get enough sleep at night? How many hours of sleep do you usually get? How much sleep do you need?

   _____

6. How do you usually feel after you exercise: energetic, relaxed, tired, or hungry?

   _____

B. Work with a group of three or four students. Make a list of seven ways to stay healthy. Write your ideas on the chart.

Ways to Stay Healthy
1. <u>Do not smoke cigarettes.</u>
2. _____
3. _____
4. _____
5. _____
6. _____
7. _____
8. _____
9. _____
10. _____

C. Compare your chart with another group's. Did you have any of the same ideas? Which ones were the same?

WRITING

Complete the paragraph about the things you do to stay healthy. The topic sentence is given. Use some of the ideas from your chart for the supporting sentences. End your paragraph with a concluding sentence.

<u>I do several things to try to stay healthy.</u> _____

_____

_____

_____

_____

A. Exchange paragraphs with a partner. Read your partner's paragraph and check *yes* or *no* to each question on the Paragraph Checklist. Then help your partner improve his/her paragraph.

Paragraph Checklist		
	YES	NO
1. Does each sentence begin with a capital letter and end with a period?	❏	❏
2. Does each new sentence begin next to the one before it?	❏	❏
3. Is there a topic sentence?	❏	❏
4. Are there at least three supporting sentences?	❏	❏
5. Is there a concluding sentence?	❏	❏

B. Use your partner's suggestions to revise your paragraph. Write your paragraph on a separate piece of paper and put it in your portfolio with the title "Staying Healthy."

On Your Own

Choose one of the following topics to write about.

1. Talk to someone in your family or one of your friends about what he/she likes to do in his/her free time. Write a paragraph about how that person spends his/her free time.

2. Talk to someone in your family or one of your friends about what he/she does to stay healthy. Write a paragraph about how that person stays healthy.

You Be the Editor

The paragraph *My Busy Sister* has six mistakes in the use of the simple present tense verbs. With a partner, find the six mistakes and correct them.

My Busy Sister

My sister Stephanie is always busy after school. As soon as she get home, she turnes on the TV. At the same time, she talk on the phone to make plans with her best friend. After she watchs TV and eats a snack, she playies computer games or IMs her friends for a while. Then she gos shopping with her friends. No wonder she's too tired to do her homework after dinner.

Real Life Writing

NOTES FOR A MESSAGE BOARD

A. Read the Wanted messages below.

WANTED

Wanted
I need a ride to New York City
on Friday, January 21.
Call Mehmet at 555-7019.

Wanted
Looking for a used tennis racket in
good condition. If you have one to sell,
please call Lucia at 555-0856.

Wanted
I'm looking for a female roommate to share
a nice apartment in a good neighborhood.
Call Leah at 555-1024.

B. Write your own message for something you want or need.

C. Read the For Sale messages below.

FOR SALE

For Sale:
Bicycle in good condition.
Call Hank at 555-6240 for details.

For Sale:
I am selling my chemistry, Spanish, and English
books from last semester. I did not write in them,
and they are in excellent condition. The teachers
are using the same books next semester. Good price!
Call Joe at 555-2280 or e-mail me at DJ@me.com.

Moving! Must Sell Cheap:
17-inch color TV. Three years old. Works
perfectly. Call Marie at 555-7124.

D. Write your own message for something you want to sell.

CHAPTER 4

Writing about Your Day

Getting Ready to Write

WRITING ABOUT YOUR DAILY ACTIVITIES

A. Look at the pictures below. They describe a typical day in the life of a man named Roberto Trevino. Find the sentence that goes with each picture from the list. Write the correct letter under each picture.

1. _____   2. _____   3. _____

4. _____   5. _____   6. _____

7. _____   8. _____

a. He teaches from 8:30 to 3:30.

b. Roberto wakes up at 7:00, eats breakfast, and gets dressed.

c. When Roberto goes to bed at midnight, he is usually very tired.

d. Then he takes the 7:45 A.M. train to the school where he is a teacher.

e. At 6:00 he eats dinner with his wife.

f. He takes the train back home at 4:00.

g. He plays the saxaphone from 8:00 to 10:00 P.M. Sometimes he sings, too.

h. At 7:30, he drives to Le Jazz Club.

B. Use the sentences about Roberto to complete a paragraph about a typical day in his life. The topic sentence and concluding sentences are given.

Roberto's days are very busy. _____

_____

_____

_____

_____

_____

_____ As you can see, Roberto has a very busy life.

Develop Your Writing Skills

USING PREPOSITIONS OF TIME

It is important to use the correct preposition when you are writing about time. Study the chart.

on	+ day of the week (I go to work *on* Monday.)
	+ day of the week + part of a day (I take an English class *on* Monday night.)
	+ a specific date (She was born *on* April 30.)
in	+ a month (She was born *in* April.)
	+ a part of the day (I do my homework *in* the evening.)
	Exception: at night (I do my homework *at* night.)
at	+ a specific time (My English class starts *at* 9:30.)
from	+ a specific time or date *to* a specific time or date (Mr. Morimoto exercises *from* 5:30 *to* 6:30 every morning.)

Complete the sentences with the correct preposition of time.

1. Do you want to go to the movies _____ Sunday afternoon?

2. She is going to the dentist _____ Monday.

3. Mohammed goes to work _____ 9:00.

4. Cheng goes to school _____ the morning.

5. I sent the e-mail _____ January 29.

6. I like to watch TV _____ night.

7. I have classes _____ 10:00 _____ 4:30.

8. The new semester starts _____ January.

9. He wakes up _____ 7:30 _____ the morning.

10. Keiko was in the hospital _____ July 3 _____ July 7.

USING FREQUENCY ADVERBS

When you want to write about how often something happens or how often you do something, you can use frequency adverbs in your sentences. The most common frequency adverbs are *always, usually, often, sometimes, rarely, seldom,* and *never.*

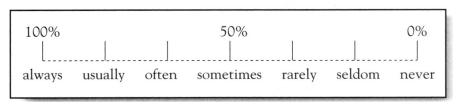

Notes about placement:

1. Frequency adverbs are used *before* regular verbs, but *after* forms of the verb **be**.

   Examples   He <u>always</u> **goes** to bed late.

   He ***is*** <u>always</u> tired in the morning.

2. *Sometimes* can also come at the beginning of a sentence.

   Examples   I <u>sometimes</u> take the bus to work.

   <u>Sometimes</u> I take the bus to work.

Adverbs	Examples
always (100% of the time)	I don't have a car. I *always* take the bus to work.
usually	He *usually* gets up at 7:00 A.M. He is *usually* on time for class.
often	We *often* go for a walk after dinner. We are *often* tired after our walk.
sometimes (50% of the time)	I *sometimes* drink coffee after dinner. I am *sometimes* late for work.
rarely	Meryl is on a diet. She *rarely* eats dessert.
seldom	Jeff *seldom* goes to bed before midnight. He is *seldom* tired before midnight.
never (0% of the time)	Suzanne is a vegetarian. She *never* eats meat.

A. Add a frequency adverb that makes each sentence true for you.

1. I _____ get up early.

2. I _____ eat breakfast at a restaurant.

3. I _____ take the bus to school or work.

4. I _____ take a nap in the afternoon.

5. I _____ make my own meals.

6. I am _____ asleep before midnight.

7. I _____ get enough sleep at night.

8. I _____ watch TV in the evening.

9. I am _____ tired after school or work.

10. I _____ take a walk after dinner.

B. Compare your sentences with a partner's. How many of them are the same?

USING *BEFORE* AND *AFTER*

Before and *after* are prepositions that can be used with nouns; for example, *before school*. You can also combine sentences with *before* and *after* to show time order.

Examples

I go to bed. I brush my teeth.

Before *I go to bed*, I brush my teeth. OR

I brush my teeth **before** *I go to bed*.

I eat lunch. I take a nap.

After *I eat lunch*, I take a nap. OR

I take a nap **after** *I eat lunch*.

Notice that we use a comma in sentences that start with *before* or *after*.

A. Combine the pairs of sentences using *before*. Use a comma.

1. I eat dinner. I wash my hands.

   _____

2. I watch TV. I do my homework.

   _____

3. I do my homework. I go to the gym.

   _____

4. I read the newspaper. I eat breakfast.

   _____

B. Combine the pairs of sentences using *after*. Use a comma.

1. I get home from work. I take my dog for a walk.

   _____

2. I eat dinner. I wash the dishes.

   _____

3. I get to school. I have coffee with my friends.

   _____

4. I read my son a story. I put him to bed.

   _____

C. Complete the sentences below.

1. After I get dressed in the morning, I _____.

2. After I get to school (work), I _____.

3. Before I do my homework, I _____.

4. Before I make dinner, I _____.

D. Compare your sentences with a partner's.

Paragraph Pointer: Using Time Order
When you write about your day, you should arrange your sentences by time order. You can use signal words to make the order clear to your reader. Here are some time order signal words: First of all Then After that Next Finally

A. Read the sentences below. Write *TS* in front of the topic sentence. Then number the supporting sentences so they are in correct time order. Finally, write the sentences in paragraph form.

1. __2__ Then he quickly gets dressed and eats breakfast.

   __TS__ Mehmet's mornings are very busy.

   __3__ At 7:45 he is outside waiting for the school bus.

   __1__ His mother wakes him up at 6:30.

   _____

   _____

   _____

   _____

2. _____ She spends every morning exercising at the gym.

   _____ After she leaves the university, she goes to work at a store from 5:00 to 9:00 P.M.

   _____ She also takes classes at the university in the afternoon.

   _____ Maria is very active during the summer.

   _____

   _____

   _____

   _____

3. _____ At 6:00 A.M. he goes to the flower market.

_____ Mr. Park owns a busy flower shop.

_____ After he buys his flowers, he works in his shop from 9:00 to 4:00.

_____ When the store closes, Mr. Park delivers flowers.

_____

_____

_____

_____

B. Read the paragraph *Lazy Sundays* and complete the exercise.

Lazy Sundays

I am usually very lazy on Sundays. I get up late, and I eat a big breakfast. After breakfast, I read the newspaper for a few hours. Sometimes I talk to my friends on the telephone. At four o'clock, I am usually hungry so I make a snack. Then I watch TV or take a nap. In the evening, I like to go out to dinner with my friends, but I am back in bed again at ten o'clock. I like to relax on Sunday so that I am ready to start my week on Monday.

1. Draw a circle around the topic sentence of the paragraph.
2. Underline the supporting sentences.
3. Draw a circle around the concluding sentence of the paragraph.

C. Rewrite the paragraph changing the word *I* to *Paulo* in the first sentence. Be sure to make all the other necessary changes.

Paulo is _____

_____

_____

_____

_____

PREWRITING

A. Talk to a partner. Ask and answer these questions. Use the words in the Word Bank to help you.

1. What do you do? (For example, are you a student? Are you a cook? Are you a nurse? Are you a businessperson?) _____

2. Where do you work or go to school? _____

3. How do you get there? _____

4. What hours do you work or study? _____

Word Bank

do homework	get up	put on makeup
do the dishes	go to bed	shave
do the laundry	go to school/work	take a shower/bath
get dressed/ undressed	make breakfast/lunch/dinner	wake up
get ready for bed	make the bed	

B. Draw simple pictures that show what you do on a typical weekday. Write a sentence to go with each picture. The first one has been done for you.

1. _I wake up at 7:00 a.m. every morning._

2. _____

3. _____

4. _____

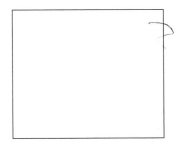

5. _____

6. _____

WRITING ABOUT YOUR DAY **45**

WRITING

Use your sentences, from page 45, to write a paragraph about a typical day in your life. Complete the following sentence and use it as your topic sentence. Use at least three adverbs of frequency in your paragraph. Add a concluding sentence at the end.

During the week, my days are very _____.
(busy/boring/interesting)

_____

_____

_____

_____

_____

_____

_____

_____

REVISING

A. Exchange paragraphs with a partner. Read your partner's paragraph and check *yes* or *no* for each question on the Paragraph Checklist. Then help your partner improve his/her paragraph.

Paragraph Checklist		
	YES	**NO**
1. Is the first word of the paragraph indented?	❑	❑
2. Does each sentence begin with a capital letter and end with a period?	❑	❑
3. Does the paragraph have a topic sentence?	❑	❑
4. Are the sentences in correct time order?	❑	❑
5. Are there at least three adverbs of frequency?	❑	❑

B. Use your partner's suggestions to revise your paragraph. Copy your revised paragraph onto a separate piece of paper, give it the title "A Typical Day in My Life," and put it in your portfolio.

Use Your Imagination

A. Discuss the cartoon with your classmates.

1. Where does this scene take place?
2. Why do you think he is frustrated?
3. Do you think the cartoon is funny? Why or why not

B. Write a paragraph about his typical workday.

You Be the Editor

Read the paragraph *A Busy Doctor.* It has five mistakes in prepositions of time. With a partner, find the mistakes and correct them. Cross out the mistakes and write the correct preposition above it.

A Busy Doctor

Dr. Gary Lesneski is an obstetrician. An obstetrician is a doctor who delivers babies. Dr. Lesneski usually gets up on 6:30 at the morning. He goes to his office at 7:00. His workdays are never typical, but they are always busy. He never knows what time a baby will decide to be born. Sometimes babies are born at the afternoon. Sometimes they are born in night. Often he has to go to the hospital in the middle of the night. He rarely sleeps through an entire night without any interruptions. Dr. Lesneski loves his work, but he looks forward to his vacation on August.

Real Life Writing

WRITING A MESSAGE ON A CARD

Do you like to send cards to your friends and family?

Look at the front of these cards. Write a two- or three-sentence message on the inside to someone you know.

HAPPY BIRTHDAY!

Dear Evelyn,

Happy Birthday! I can't believe you're 21! I hope you have a great day and a wonderful year.

Love,
Aunt Susan

A New House

SOLD

Get Well Soon!

CHAPTER 5

Writing Descriptions

Getting Ready to Write

WRITING ABOUT PEOPLE

A. Look at the people in the pictures. Match the description to the correct picture. Write the correct letter under each picture. Use the words in the Word Banks on the next page to help you.

1. _____ 2. _____ 3. _____ 4. _____ 5. _____

   a. Mr. Wilcox is a tall, thin middle-aged man. He is bald but has a black mustache. He wears big glasses. He is wearing a blue jacket and a striped tie. He is carrying a briefcase and an umbrella.

   b. Sally is a slender young woman of average height. She has long straight blond hair with bangs that touch the top of her glasses. She is wearing a short wool skirt with a v-neck sweater and leather boots.

   c. Dennis is a short young man with a round face and curly red hair. He has big brown eyes, freckles, and a dimple in his chin. He is wearing his favorite T-shirt and shorts. He has a backpack.

   d. Tom is a good-looking teenager. He is average height and weight. He has straight black hair and green eyes. He is wearing a sweatshirt and jeans. He is also wearing a baseball cap and a new pair of white sneakers.

   e. Juanita is an attractive young woman. She has long wavy brown hair and big beautiful eyes. Today she's got her hair in a ponytail. She is wearing a striped pantsuit and a black turtleneck. She's got on a silver necklace and long earrings.

Physical Characteristics Word Bank					
Hair	**Eyes**	**Height**	**Build**	**Face**	**Age**
bald black blond brown curly dark long ponytail red short straight wavy	blue brown dark green hazel	average short tall	average heavy medium slender small stocky strong thin	beard dimple freckles mole mustache	middle-aged old teenaged young

Clothing Word Bank				
blazer shirt/blouse sweater sweatshirt T-shirt turtleneck vest	bracelet earrings glasses necklace ring watch	dress jeans pants shorts skirt suit sweatpants	boots pumps sandals shoes sneakers socks	baseball cap belt coat gloves hat purse scarf umbrella

B. Write a short description of these people. Use the words in the Word Banks to help you.

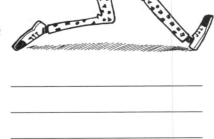

1. _____

_____

_____

_____

2. _____

_____

_____

_____

Develop Your Writing Skills

ADJECTIVES

An adjective is a word that describes a noun. When you write descriptions, you should use adjectives. For example, in the sentence "She has long black hair." the words *long* and *black* are adjectives that describe the noun *hair*. They answer the question, "What kind of hair?"

Here are some rules to remember about using adjectives in English:

> 1. Adjectives have the same form when they describe singular or plural nouns.
>
>   **Example:** She is wearing a **new** jacket. They are wearing **new** jackets.
>
> 2. Adjectives come before nouns.
>
>   **Example:** He has **brown** eyes. They are wearing **old** sneakers.
>
> 3. Adjectives can come after the verb *be*.
>
>   **Example:** His eyes are **brown**. Their sneakers are **old**.

A. Underline the adjectives in the descriptions on page 49.

B. Read what a student wrote to describe her appearance. Underline the adjectives.

> My name is Jenny Marsh. I am tall and thin. I have long black hair and big brown eyes. I wear glasses. Today I am wearing old blue jeans and a soft yellow sweater. I have on a brown belt and white sneakers.

PREWRITING

Answer these questions about yourself.

1. What color eyes and hair do you have?

   _____

2. Are you tall, short, or average height?

   _____

3. What are you wearing?

   _____

WRITING

A. Use the answers to the Prewriting questions on page 51 to write a description of yourself on a separate piece of paper. Do not put your name on the paper. Fold your paper in half and give it to your teacher. Your teacher will give your paper to another student who will try to guess who wrote the description.

B. When your partner returns your description to you, copy it on the lines below. Add a topic sentence.

My name is _____ . _____

_____

_____

_____

_____

REVISING

A. Exchange paragraphs with a partner. Read your partner's description and check *yes* or *no* for each question on the Paragraph Checklist. Then help your partner improve his/her description.

Paragraph Checklist		
	YES	NO
1. Is the first word of the paragraph indented?	❏	❏
2. Does each sentence begin with a capital letter and end with a period?	❏	❏
3. Does the paragraph have a topic sentence?	❏	❏
4. Are there at least five adjectives to support the topic?	❏	❏

B. Use your partner's suggestions to revise your paragraph. Then copy it onto a separate piece of paper. Give it the title "What I Look Like" and put it in your portfolio.

Paragraph Pointer: Using Examples

One way to develop a paragraph is to use examples to support your topic sentence. Use "For instance" or "For example" when you give an example.

Complete the sentences with examples.

1. Several of my friends are athletic. *For instance,* _____, _____, and _____ are all good at sports.

2. I love to travel. There are many places I want to visit. *For example,* I would love to see _____, _____, and _____.

3. Many inventions have made our lives easier. *For example,* _____, _____, and _____ have all made our day-to-day activities easier.

DESCRIBING SOMEONE'S CHARACTER

A. Read the paragraph below and talk about the questions that follow with a partner.

I am a very organized person. For example, I keep my closet very neat. All of my clothes and shoes are arranged by color. I also organize the books in my bookcase by topic. I keep my CDs in alphabetical order so that they are always easy to find. I put all of my important papers in a file in my desk so nothing ever gets lost. My husband makes fun of me and says that I am too organized. However, I never lose anything, and my husband is always looking for something.

1. What is the topic sentence?
2. What examples does the author give to support the idea that the author is an organized person?

B. Rewrite the paragraph changing the word *I* to *Yoko* in the first sentence.

Yoko is a _____

_____

_____

_____

_____

PREWRITING

A. Think of a person you know well such as a friend, relative, neighbor, classmate, or teacher. Circle one adjective from the Word Bank that describes the person.

Word Bank

ambitious	dependable	hardworking	messy	quiet	shy
artistic	energetic	helpful	neat	responsible	social
boring	enthusiastic	honest	optimistic	selfish	studious
brave	friendly	jealous	organized	sensitive	talkative
competitive	funny	kind	patient	serious	thrifty
creative	generous	lazy			

B. Write the topic sentence for a paragraph about the person. Include both the name of the person and the adjective you chose.

Example: My brother is a very lazy person.

C. Make a list of at least three examples that support your topic sentence.

Example: He sits on the couch all weekend watching TV.

1. _____

2. _____

3. _____

WRITING

Use your list as a guide to write a paragraph. Remember to start with your topic sentence. Try to include at least three examples.

_____

_____

_____

_____

_____

REVISING

A. Exchange paragraphs with a partner. Read your partner's paragraph and check *yes* or *no* for each question on the Paragraph Checklist. Then help your partner improve his/her description.

Paragraph Checklist		
	YES	**NO**
1. Does the paragraph have a topic sentence?	❏	❏
2. Does the topic sentence give the name of the person and an adjective that describes him/her?	❏	❏
3. Are there at least three examples to support the topic?	❏	❏

B. Use your partner's suggestions to revise your paragraph. Then copy it onto a separate piece of paper. Give it the title "A _____ Person" and put it in your portfolio.

On Your Own

On a separate piece of paper, write a paragraph about your own character, using the Word Bank on page 54. Give at least three examples to support your topic sentence. After your teacher has read your paragraph, copy it over, and put it in your portfolio with the title "More about Me."

DESCRIBING THINGS

A. Discuss the pictures below from The International Gift Shop catalog with a partner. Match the name of the item with the correct picture. Write the name of the item on the line.

Chinese rug   flowered plate   leather gloves   necklace   Turkish towels

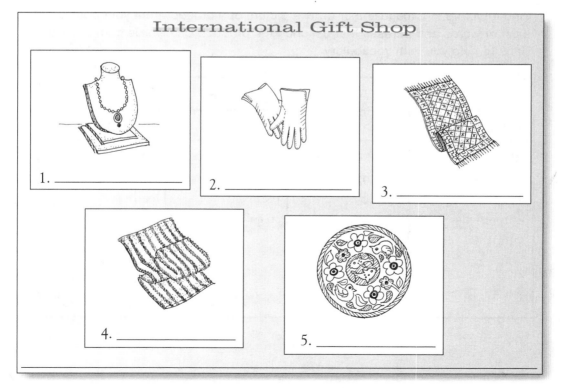

International Gift Shop

1. _____

2. _____

3. _____

4. _____

5. _____

B. Read the following description of each item. Circle the adjectives in each description.

1. These 100% cotton Turkish towels have blue and white stripes. They are very large and soft. They are so thick you will want to use them at home and at the beach. You can order two for only $45. (Item 001)

2. This beautiful necklace was made in Korea. It will make a nice gift for a special person. You can order this pretty 22-inch necklace for $90. (Item 002)

3. These brown leather gloves are made in Brazil and will keep your hands warm in winter. The leather is soft and smooth. You can order a pair of these attractive gloves in size small, medium, or large. Buy them for yourself, or give them as a gift for $25. (Item 003)

4. This round plate was hand-painted in Mexico. The interesting design has pictures of flowers, trees, birds, and fish. The bright colors look nice in any room. We are offering it to you for only $20, so order it right away. (Item 004)

5. This rectangular silk and wool rug was made by hand in China. It is three feet wide and six feet long. The geometric pattern is based on the Chinese symbol for happiness. You can own this beautiful rug for a special price of $530. (Item 005)

Paragraph Pointer: Using Details in Your Writing

The key to writing a good description is using specific details. When you describe what someone or something looks like, use lots of details in the supporting sentences so your readers can form a picture in their minds.

PREWRITING

Find a picture in a magazine or draw a picture of a product from your country. Make a list of words and phrases that describe the product. Use words from the Word Bank to help you with vocabulary.

Description Word Bank			
Opinion	Shape	Design	Material
attractive	oval	flowered	cotton
beautiful	rectangular	geometric	gold
bright	square	plain	leather
interesting		striped	plastic
pretty			silk
soft			silver
			wood
			wool

Picture of a Product from My Country

_____ _____
_____ _____
_____ _____
_____ _____

WRITING

Use the list you wrote as a guide to describe your product for The International Gift Shop catalog. Begin with a sentence that gives the name of the product and the country it is from. Use at least five adjectives. Don't forget to include the price of your product.

_____
_____
_____
_____

REVISING

A. Exchange your description with a partner. Read your partner's description and check *yes* or *no* for each question on the Paragraph Checklist. Then help your partner improve his/her description.

Paragraph Checklist		
	YES	**NO**
1. Is the name of the product and the country it is from stated in the first sentence?	❏	❏
2. Does the description look like the picture of the product?	❏	❏
3. Are there enough adjectives to describe nouns?	❏	❏
4. Are the adjectives in the correct order?	❏	❏
5. Does the paragraph have a topic sentence?	❏	❏
6. Is the price given?	❏	❏

B. Use your partner's suggestions to revise your description. Then copy it onto a separate piece of paper. Give it the title "A Product from _____" and put it in your portfolio.

On Your Own

Draw a picture of your national flag. Write a paragraph called "My National Flag" that describes what your flag looks like. Include the colors, shapes, design, etc. If any of these things has a special meaning, you can write about that, too. Share your description with your classmates. Give your description a title and put it in your portfolio.

Use Your Imagination

WRITING ABOUT CARS

Study the words in the Word Bank.

Car Parts Word Bank

INTERIOR

accelerator	CD player/radio	emergency brake	rearview mirror
airbag	clutch	gearshift	seatbelt
brake	dashboard	ignition	steering wheel
bucket seat			

EXTERIOR

bumper	hood	side mirror	trunk	windshield
gas tank	license plate	taillight	turn signals	windshield wipers
headlight	roof	tire	wheel covers	

A. Think about what cars will be like in the future. Use your imagination to write a paragraph about cars of the future. For example, do you think that they will be bigger or smaller? Will they still run on gasoline? What will dashboards look like? Will cars need bumpers? Where will the trunk be? How many tires will cars have? Will humans have to drive them?

B. Exchange paragraphs with a partner. Suggest changes that you think will make the paragraph better.

C. Rewrite your paragraph on a separate piece of paper and put it in your portfolio with the title "Cars of the Future."

You Be the Editor

Read the paragraph *A Birthday Gift.* It has five mistakes in the use of adjectives. With a partner, find the five mistakes and correct them.

A Birthday Gift

My brother's birthday is next week, and I want to buy him a news sweater. In a catalog I saw one that is made in Canada. I think he will like it. It's a striped sweater blue. My brother has eyes blue so it will look nice on him. The sweater is made of soft wool, so it is warms. It is a sweater that fits loosely, so it comfortable is to wear. He can wear it to work or on the weekends. I'm so happy I had this idea, and I think my brother will be happy, too!

Real Life Writing

FILLING OUT AN ORDER FORM

You want to order something from The International Gift Shop catalog on page 55. Complete the order form below.

THE INTERNATIONAL GIFT SHOP		**Send To:**	Name			
ORDER TOLL FREE 1–800–371–2311			Address			
			City			
			State		Zip	
			Country			

Item Number	Quantity	Item Description	Color	Gift Wrap	Price	Total Price
				Yes/No		

Payment Method						
☐ Check		☐ Credit Card		Merchandise Total		
				$2.00 Shipping Charge		
Card Account Number			Month Year	TOTAL		

Signature _____

CHAPTER 6

Writing about Places

Getting Ready to Write

DESCRIBING A ROOM

A. Look at the picture of a student's bedroom and underline the adjectives in the paragraph *A Cozy Bedroom.*

A Cozy Bedroom

My bedroom is small but cozy. There are two windows so my room is usually bright and sunny. I have a desk for my laptop computer. All the books I need to use while I am studying are in the bookcase. My bed is across from the desk. It is not big, but it is comfortable. Above the bed, there is a painting of a bowl of fruit that I did in my art class. It's not very good, but I love the bright colors. I also have an old dresser that belonged to my grandmother. There are several photographs of my family on top of it. I enjoy spending time in my bedroom.

B. Look at the pictures of the three dormitory rooms. In small groups, discuss each picture and make a list of the things in each room. Use the Word Bank to help you.

Word Bank

art supplies	clock	fishing gear	phone	tennis racquet
bed	closet	hockey stick	poster	TV
bedspread	computer	ice skates	Rollerblades	vase
bookcase	curtains	lamp	rug	VCR
books	desk	nightstand	skis	wastebasket
chair	dresser	painting	stereo	window

Room 1

_____

_____

_____

_____

_____

_____

_____

Room 2

_____

_____

_____

_____

_____

_____

Room 3

_____

_____

_____

_____

_____

_____

C. What adjectives would you use to describe each room? Use the Word Bank to help you. Try to add some other words.

```
                    Word Bank

        clean      messy      organized

        cluttered  neat       small

        cozy       orderly    sunny

        large
```

Room 1   **Room 2**   **Room 3**

messy

Develop Your Writing Skills

THERE IS AND THERE ARE

When you describe a place, you can use _there is_ and _there are_. Look at these examples:

There is a big window in the classroom.
There are lots of windows in the classroom.

There is one computer in my office.
There are many computers in the library.

> Remember these rules:
>
> • Use "there is" with single nouns.
>
> • Use "there are" with plural countable nouns.
>
> • The subject comes after the verb:
>   There is a <u>dictionary</u> on the table.
>   There are <u>some books</u> on the table.

A. Underline the sentences with _there is_ and _there are_ in the paragraph _A Cozy Bedroom_ on page 60.

B. Work with a partner. Write two sentences about each of the rooms on page 61 using _there is_ or _there are_.

Room 1

1. _____

2. _____

Room 2

1. _____

2. _____

Room 3

1. _____

2. _____

PREPOSITIONS OF PLACE

When you want to explain where something is located, you need to use the correct preposition. The prepositions in the box will help you describe where items are located in relation to other items.

above	beside	in	in front of	on
behind	between	in back of	next to	under

A. Look at the following pictures. Then complete the sentences with the correct prepositions from the list above.

1. There are three pictures _____*above*_____ the couch. The coffee table is _____*in front of*_____ the couch. There are some flowers _____*in*_____ the vase _____*on*_____ the coffee table.

2. There are lots of books _____ the bookcase. The fax machine is _____ a table _____ the bookcase and desk. There is a computer _____ the desk. The wastebasket is _____ the desk.

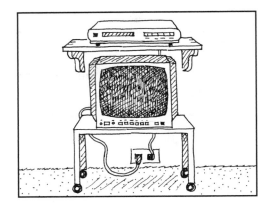

3. The DVD player is _____ the shelf _____ the TV. There is an electrical outlet _____ the TV.

B. Look at the picture on page 65. Practice using prepositions of place by adding each new item to the picture. Then compare your picture with one of your classmates' pictures.

1. Draw a bowl of fruit in front of the grandmother.
2. Draw a dog under the table.
3. Draw a ball beside the dog.
4. Draw a toy next to the ball.
5. Draw a clock on the wall behind the grandfather.
6. Draw a vase between the candles on the table.
7. Draw a flower in the vase.
8. Draw a cake on the long table behind the mother.
9. Draw a painting on the wall above the long table.

Paragraph Pointer: Paragraph Unity

When you write a paragraph, all of the sentences must support the main idea stated in the topic sentence. This is called paragraph unity. Do not include sentences that do not relate to the topic sentence.

A. Read the paragraph below.

My living room has things from all over the world in it. For example, I bought the antique rug in China. The pillows on the couch are made from fabric I got on my trip to India. The three paintings on the walls are by a Cuban artist. My cat loves to sit on the big red chair next to the couch. My coffee table is covered with glass paper weights I collect from Scotland. Finally, my bookshelves are filled with travel books from all the countries I have visited.

All of the sentences except one support the main idea stated in the topic sentence. The fact that the cat loves to sit on the big red chair does not relate to the idea that the things in the room are from all over the world. It should not be included in the paragraph.

B. Now, read the paragraph *A Messy Bedroom* and underline the topic sentence. Then find the two sentences that do not support the main idea and cross them out.

A Messy Bedroom

My son's bedroom is always messy. For example, he rarely makes his bed or hangs up his clothes. There are usually piles of clothes on the floor and chair. His schoolbooks and papers are all over his desk. His favorite book is *One Hundred Years of Solitude*. The top of his dresser is covered with CDs, soda cans, and magazines. I bought the dresser for him at a used furniture store. I wish he would clean up his room!

PREWRITING

A. Think about your bedroom or dormitory room. Describe it to a partner. Discuss the things you like and don't like about your room. Ask and answer the questions.

1. What size is your room?
2. What adjectives would you use to describe it?
3. What pieces of furniture do you have in your room?
4. Are there any windows? Is it sunny or dark?
5. Do you like your room? Why or why not.

B. Draw a simple picture of your room.

WRITING

Write a paragraph that describes your room. Use at least three prepositions of place. Also write at least one sentence with *there is* and one sentence with *there are.* Remember to begin with a topic sentence.

_____

_____

_____

_____

_____

_____

_____

_____

_____

_____

REVISING

A. Exchange paragraphs with a partner. Read your partner's paragraph and check *yes* or *no* to each question on the Paragraph Checklist. Then help your partner improve his/her paragraph.

Paragraph Checklist		
	YES	**NO**
1. Does the paragraph begin with a topic sentence?	❏	❏
2. Does the paragraph have enough details?	❏	❏
3. Does the paragraph include sentences with *there is* and *there are?*	❏	❏
4. Are there at least three prepositions of place?	❏	❏
5. Are there any sentences that do not belong?	❏	❏

B. Use your partner's suggestions to revise your paragraph. Copy your revised paragraph onto a separate piece of paper, give it the title "My Room," and put it in your portfolio.

WRITING ABOUT YOUR HOME

Read the following letter.

January 2

Dear Mom,

    I just moved into my new apartment. It is on the second floor of a building near school. The thing I like most about the apartment is that it's very sunny. There are big windows in every room. It has a large living room with a fireplace. There are bookcases on two walls. The kitchen is small, but the appliances are new. There is a long hall next to the kitchen that leads to the bedroom and bathroom. There is new carpeting in the bedroom. The only problem is that the closet in the bedroom is very small. I can't wait for you to visit me.

Love,
Sema

PREWRITING

Think about the place where you live. Describe your house, apartment, or room to a partner. Discuss the things you like and don't like about the place. Ask and answer these questions:

1. Where do you live?
2. How big is your home? How many rooms does it have? What size are the rooms?
3. Is your home old or new?
4. Is it sunny or dark? Are there lots of windows?
5. Do you like your home? Why or why not?

Write about your home in a letter to a friend or relative in the space below. Use the letter on page 68 as a guide.

_____ (date)

Dear _____ ,

Love,

_____

REVISING

After your teacher has read your letter, use any suggestions to revise your letter, copy it over, and put it in your portfolio under the title "My Home."

WRITING ABOUT YOUR HOMETOWN

Read the paragraph *My Hometown* and cross out the sentence that doesn't belong.

My Hometown

I am from Vancouver, a large city in the southwest corner of Canada near the Pacific Ocean. Vancouver is a beautiful city that is surrounded by water and mountains. Vancouver has a mild climate, even in winter. Now I live in Florida, and it is often very hot and humid. Vancouver is an important center for business. It is the busiest port city in Canada, and it is a center of mining, software, and biotechnology. We also have a huge tourist industry. Vancouver is safe and clean, and it has natural beauty as well as many historic, cultural, and recreational opportunities. I love my city and I think you will, too. Please come visit Vancouver!

PREWRITING

A. Describe your hometown to a partner. Use the words in the Word Bank to help you.

> **Word Bank**
>
> | architecture | crime | polluted |
> | bridges | cultural attractions | population |
> | capitol | industry | port |
> | city | modern | safe |
> | clean | night life | sports |
> | climate | parks | town |

B. Make a list of the information about your hometown that you want to include in your paragraph.

_____

_____

_____

_____

_____

_____

_____

WRITING

Complete the topic sentence below. Then use the information on your list to write a paragraph. Try to include at least three adjectives in your paragraph.

My hometown, _____ , is a _____ place.

_____

_____

_____

_____

_____

_____

REVISING

A. Exchange paragraphs with a partner. Read your partner's paragraph and check *yes* or *no* to each question on the Paragraph Checklist. Then help your partner improve his/her paragraph.

Paragraph Checklist

	YES	NO
1. Does the paragraph begin with a topic sentence?	❏	❏
2. Does the paragraph have enough details?	❏	❏
3. Are there at least three adjectives?	❏	❏
4. Are there any sentences that do not belong?	❏	❏

B. Use your partner's suggestions to revise your paragraph. After your teacher has read your paragraph, copy it over and put it in your portfolio with the title "My Hometown."

WRITING A LETTER

A. Write a letter to a friend who is coming to visit you. Make a list of the places to go and things to do.

Places to Go

_____

_____

_____

_____

_____

Things to Do

_____

_____

_____

_____

_____

B. The letter has been started for you. Complete the beginning of the letter and then finish it.

_____ (date)

Dear _____,

I was so happy when you called to tell me you were planning to come

to _____ to visit me. There are lots of places to go

and things to see and do here. We can _____

_____. _____

_____

_____

_____

_____

_____

Love,

_____

On Your Own

DESCRIBING A PICTURE

A. Write three sentences that describe the photograph. Use a preposition in each sentence.

1. _____

2. _____

3. _____

B. Use the sentences you wrote to write a description of the picture.

_____

_____

_____

_____

_____

_____

_____

_____

Use Your Imagination

WRITING A HAIKU

Haiku is a very old form of poetry from Japan. Haiku poems are usually about nature.

The form of a haiku is always the same. It contains three lines:

> The first line has five syllables.
>
> The second line has seven syllables.
>
> The third line has five syllables.

Here are some examples that students have written.

Look up in the sky
See the blue birds flying high
Over the ocean

—Vasakorn Bhadranavik

Noisy rain has stopped
White snow covers everything
Silent night has come

—Kazu Karasawa

The birds of passage
Are taking a winter's rest
Ready to go south

—Fumihiko Suita

A. Choose a season and a scene from nature that you would like to write about. Think about the picture that you want to create in your readers' minds. Then follow the steps to write your own haiku.

Season: _____

Scene from nature: _____

_____

B. 1. Decide what your first line will be. Work on the words until you have exactly five syllables. Write it on the first line in the box.
2. Write your second line. Remember that it must contain seven syllables.
3. Write your third line. Make sure it contains five syllables.

My Haiku
_____
_____
_____

C. Exchange your haiku with a partner. Make sure you understand your partner's haiku. Make sure the syllable count is correct for each line.

D. Rewrite your haiku on a separate sheet of paper. Illustrate your haiku as in the examples and display it in your classroom. When your haiku is returned to you, put it in your portfolio with the title "My Haiku."

You Be the Editor

Read the paragraph *A Popular Place to Vacation.* It has five mistakes in the use of *there is* and *there are*. With a partner, find the mistakes and correct them. There is also one sentence that does not belong. Find the sentence and cross it out.

A Popular Place to Vacation

Honolulu is a great place to go for a family vacation because there is many things to do and see. First of all, there is beautiful beaches that are perfect for people who like water sports. For example, Waikiki Beach is one of the most famous surfing areas in the world. Surfing can be dangerous. The hikers in your family will find lots of challenges. For instance, there are a big volcano called Diamond Head that is right in Honolulu. The view from the top of Diamond Head is spectacular. The shopping is also fabulous. Many stores there are to choose from. Some members of your family might enjoy going to a hula show or a luau dinner in the evening. It is also an aquarium you can visit. It's no wonder that Hawaii is one of the most popular vacation destinations in the world.

Real Life Writing

ADDRESSING AN ENVELOPE

A. Look at the sample envelope.

Toby Boxer
52 Walden Street
Ames, IA 50010

Ms. Charlotte Brown
234 Benefit Street
Providence, RI 02912

B. Address the envelope for your letter to your friend on page 71. Put your name and address in the upper left corner. Then put the person's name and address in the middle.

WRITING A POSTCARD

A. Read the following postcard that was sent from Rio de Janeiro, Brazil. It shows the correct form for writing and addressing a postcard.

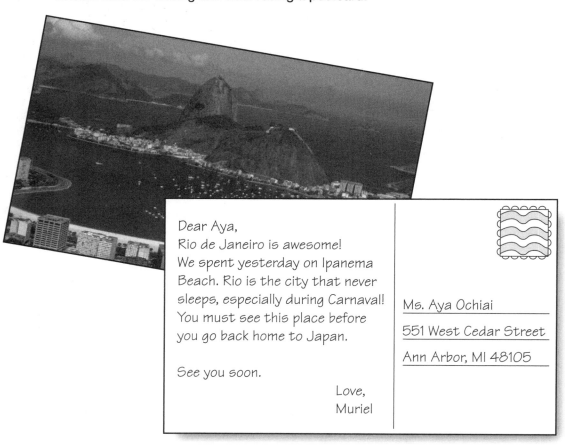

Dear Aya,
Rio de Janeiro is awesome!
We spent yesterday on Ipanema
Beach. Rio is the city that never
sleeps, especially during Carnaval!
You must see this place before
you go back home to Japan.

See you soon.

Love,
Muriel

Ms. Aya Ochiai
551 West Cedar Street
Ann Arbor, MI 48105

B. Use the space below to draw a simple picture that shows a place you have visited. Then write a message to a friend or relative. Address the postcard correctly.

CHAPTER 7

Writing Instructions

Getting Ready to Write

WRITING STEPS IN A PROCESS

A. Look at the six pictures below. They show the steps involved in making a yogurt milkshake. Find the sentence from the list below that goes with each picture. Match the sentence to the correct picture.

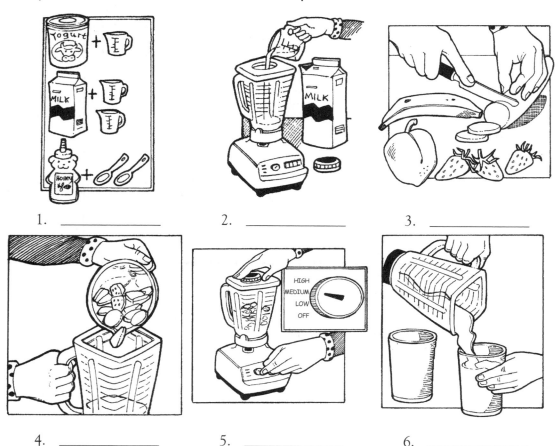

1. _____   2. _____   3. _____

4. _____   5. _____   6. _____

a. Then cut up some fresh fruit such as bananas, peaches, mangoes, or strawberries.
b. First, get out one cup of yogurt, two cups of milk, and two tablespoons of honey.
c. Add the fruit to the yogurt, milk, and honey in the blender.
d. Pour the yogurt, milk, and honey into a blender.
e. Finally, pour the milkshake into glasses and enjoy your nutritious snack.
f. Put the top on the blender and blend on medium for two minutes.

B. Use the sentences to complete a paragraph about how to make a yogurt milkshake.

How to Make a Yogurt Milkshake

When you want a delicious and healthy snack, try this yogurt milkshake.

_____

_____

_____

_____

Develop Your Writing Skills

PLURAL NOUNS

Most English nouns have a singular and plural form. Study the charts below to see how to form plural nouns.

Forming the plural of nouns

Type of Noun	Forming Plural	Examples
Most nouns	Add an _s_	banana/bananas cup/cups snack/snacks
Nouns that end in _s_, _ss_, _x_, _sh_, and _ch_	Add _es_	glass/glasses class/classes tax/taxes wish/wishes lunch/lunches
Nouns that end in a consonant + _y_	Change the _y_ to _i_ and add _es_	berry/berries city/cities family/families

There are other rules for the plural forms, but these are the most common:

Type of Noun	Forming Plural	Examples
Nouns that end in *o*	Add *es*	mango/mangoes potato/potatoes tomato/tomatoes volcano/volcanoes
Nouns that end in *f*	Change *f* to *v* and add *es*	half/halves wolf/wolves loaf/loaves Exception: roof/roofs
Nouns that end in *fe*	Change *f* to *v* and add *s*	knife/knives life/lives wife/wives

In addition, there are plural forms that do not follow rules. They are irregular plural nouns:

man/men   woman/women   child/children   person/people

foot/feet   tooth/teeth   mouse/mice   radio/radios

Look at your paragraph *How to Make a Yogurt Milkshake* and underline the plural nouns.

Paragraph Pointer: Organizing Steps in a Process

When you want to tell someone how to do something, the first thing you need to do is make a list of the steps in the process. Then you should arrange the steps according to time order. When you write your paragraph, use signal words to make the order of the steps clear to the reader. Here are some examples of time-order signal words:

first, second, third

first of all,

then,

after that,

next,

finally,

Complete the following paragraphs using time-order signal words.

1. It is easy to get a good picture of your cat if you follow these steps. _____, give your cat something to eat. When she is full, move your cat to a sunny window. _____, rub your cat's back for a few minutes until she falls asleep. Do not make any loud noises. As soon as she wakes up, get in position and have your camera ready. _____, take the picture as she yawns and stretches.

2. In order to get a driver's license in the United States you need to follow these steps. _____, go to the Department of Motor Vehicles in the state where you live and fill out an application. _____, study for and take a written test on the traffic signs and driving laws. You also have to take and pass a vision test. _____, take a road test with an examiner who will make sure that you can drive safely. Once you pass the road test, you will get your driver's license.

IMPERATIVE SENTENCES

When you tell someone how to do something you can use imperative sentences. Imperative sentences begin with the base form of a verb and end with a period. Imperative sentences are different from regular sentences because they do not have a subject. Look at the examples. Notice that each one begins with a verb.

Examples

Give your cat something to eat.

Go to the Department of Motor Vehicles in the state where you live and fill out an application.

For negative imperative forms use: *Do* + *not* (OR *Don't*) + base form of the verb.

Do not make any loud noises.

Look back at your paragraph *How to Make a Yogurt Milkshake.* **Underline the imperative sentences you used.**

How to Remove an Ink Stain

A. With a partner discuss the pictures below. They show how to remove an ink stain from a piece of clothing. Read the list of steps that follows and number the steps so they are in the correct order.

1.
2.
3.
4.
5.

_____ Then spray the stain with hair spray.

_____ After that, rub the stain gently with a clean cloth.

_____ First, put a paper towel under the stain.

_____ Finally, wash the piece of clothing as usual.

_____ Continue rubbing until the stain is completely gone.

B. Add the topic sentence below and then use the steps to complete the paragraph.

This is what you need to do to remove an ink stain from clothing.

_____

_____

_____

_____

How to Stop a Nosebleed

A. With a partner talk about the pictures that show how to stop a nosebleed. Then read the list of steps that follow. Put the steps in the correct order.

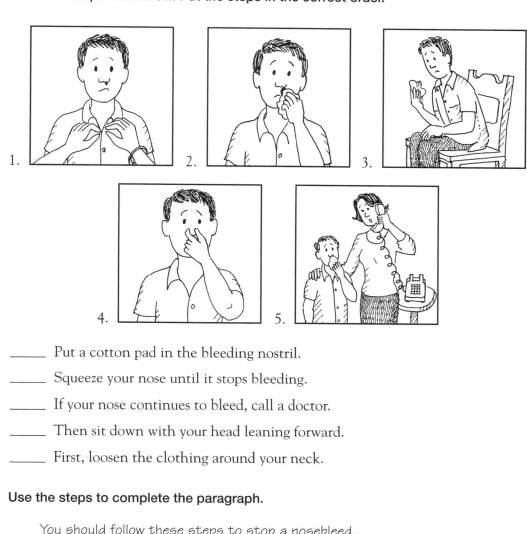

_____ Put a cotton pad in the bleeding nostril.

_____ Squeeze your nose until it stops bleeding.

_____ If your nose continues to bleed, call a doctor.

_____ Then sit down with your head leaning forward.

_____ First, loosen the clothing around your neck.

B. Use the steps to complete the paragraph.

You should follow these steps to stop a nosebleed. _____

_____

_____

_____

_____

How to Clean Silver Jewelry

A. Look at the six pictures. They show how to clean silver jewelry. Write a sentence for each picture.

1.
2.
3.
4.
5.
6.

1. First of all, put a piece of aluminum foil in a pot. _____

2. _____

3. _____

4. _____

5. _____

6. _____

B. Use your sentences to write a paragraph. The topic sentence is given. Be sure to include signal words.

Here is an easy way to clean silver jewelry. _____

_____

_____

_____

_____

PREWRITING

A. Choose one of the following topics to write about.

- How to give your pet a bath
- How to pack for a weekend trip
- How to make a good salad
- How to fall asleep
- How to mend a broken heart
- How to cure the hiccups
- How to treat a cold
- How to convert from Celsius to Fahrenheit or metric to American measurements

B. Make a list of all the steps in the process. Then put the steps in the correct time order.

_____

_____

_____

_____

_____

_____

_____

_____

_____

WRITING

Write a paragraph giving instructions. Use the list of steps as a guide. Remember to begin with a topic sentence that states the process you are describing. Also be sure to include some signal words to help guide your reader.

_____

_____

_____

_____

_____

REVISING

A.   Exchange paragraphs with a partner. Read your partner's paragraph and check *yes* or *no* to each question on the Paragraph Checklist. Then help your partner improve his/her instructions.

Paragraph Checklist		
	YES	**NO**
1. Is there a topic sentence?	❏	❏
2. Are the sentences in the correct time order?	❏	❏
3. Are there signal words to help guide the reader?	❏	❏

B.   Write a title for your paragraph. Share your paragraph with your classmates. Put your instruction paragraph in your portfolio.

On Your Own

Choose one of the following topics and write a process paragraph on a separate piece of paper. Give your paragraph a title and put it in your portfolio.

- How to clean something (your room, your car, etc.)
- How to fix something (a flat tire, a broken vase, etc.)
- How to cook or bake something
- How to play something (checkers, soccer, etc.)
- One of the other paragraph topics from the list on page 85

You Be the Editor

Read the paragraph *Driving on Wet Roads*. It has six mistakes in singular and plural nouns. With a partner, find the mistakes and correct them.

Driving on Wet Roads

Driving on wet or slippery roads can be dangerous. If you are like many mens and womans, you might not know what to do. When your car starts to skid, these tip may be helpful. First of all, slowly take your right feet off the gas pedal. Then, turn the steering wheel slowly and only as much as necessary to keep your car wheels on the road. Next, if you have to use your brakes, squeeze them firmly, and then take your foot off the pedal. Finally, do not try to stop or turn quickly. Knowing how to drive on slippery roads can save many lifes.

Real Life Writing

WRITING A RECIPE CARD

A. Write a recipe card for one of your favorite dishes. Fill out the recipe card below. First make a list of the ingredients. Then write the instructions for how to prepare the dish. Use the words in the Word Bank below to help you.

Word Bank

bake	chop	cut	grill	mix	sauté
boil	combine	fry	heat	peel	simmer
broil	cook	garnish	melt	pour	stir

_____
(name of dish)

Ingredients: _____

_____

_____

_____

_____

Instructions: _____

_____

_____

B. Prepare the dish and bring it to class to share with your classmates. Put your recipe card in your portfolio.

CHAPTER 8

Writing a Narrative

Getting Ready to Write

WRITING A STORY

Read the story *My First Camping Trip* and number the pictures so they tell the story in the correct time order.

My First Camping Trip

My first camping trip was not at all what I expected. My brother and I packed our car Friday afternoon and drove five hours to a beautiful campsite in Maine. I thought it would be hard to put up our tent, but it was easy. It only took a few minutes. We made a fire and cooked a delicious dinner over the fire. We enjoyed a beautiful sunset. Then we went into the tent and fell asleep surrounded by the peace and quiet of the trees. There were no bugs and no bears. It rained a little in the night, but we were warm and dry in our tent. When we woke up, the sun was out and we took a walk along the river. What a surprise. I like camping!

_____

_____

_____

_____

_____

_____

Develop Your Writing Skills

PAST TENSE VERBS

Many English verbs are regular and form the past tense by adding *ed* to the base form.

Example   pack—pack**ed**.

Study the spelling rules below for forming the past tense of regular verbs.

Rules		Examples
1. For verbs ending in: one vowel + *y*, two consonants two vowels + one consonant	} add *ed*	enjoy—enjoyed walk—walked need—needed
2. For verbs ending in a consonant + *e*, add *d*		arrive—arrived
3. For verbs ending in a consonant + *y*, change the *y* to *i* and add *ed*.		study—studied
4. For verbs ending in one vowel + one consonant, double the final consonant and add *ed*		plan—planned

There are also many common verbs in English that are irregular. Study these common past tense forms of irregular verbs.

Verb	Past Tense Form	Verb	Past Tense Form
become	became	leave	left
begin	began	make	made
bring	brought	say	said
build	built	see	saw
come	came	sell	sold
drive	drove	speak	spoke
fall	fell	spend	spent
find	found	take	took
fly	flew	teach	taught
get	got	tell	told
give	gave	think	thought
go	went	wake	woke
have	had		

Note: Refer to Appendix 2 on page 120 for an additional list of irregular verbs and their past tense forms.

A. Underline the past tense verbs in *My First Camping Trip* on page 88.

B. Read the paragraph *A Computer Revolution* and fill in the blanks with the correct past tense of the verb. Compare your answers with a partner's.

A Computer Revolution

Early computers were very different from the computers you use today. They were very big, expensive, and difficult to use. In 1976, everything _____ (change). That year two young friends named
<u>1.</u>

Steve Wozniak and Steve Jobs _____ (invent) something
<u>2.</u>

new and _____ (start) a computer revolution. They
<u>3.</u>

_____ (design) and _____ (build) the first small,
<u>4.</u>   <u>5.</u>

inexpensive personal computer. They _____ (call) it the
<u>6.</u>

Apple I. They _____ (sell) 600 Apple I computers for
<u>7.</u>

$666 apiece. The next year, the two Steves _____ (develop) the
<u>8.</u>

Apple II. It was one of the first personal computers with color graphics and a keyboard. The Apple II was a huge success. It _____ (make)
<u>9.</u>

computer history because it was the first easy-to-use personal computer.

Steve Jobs _____ (believe) in bringing computer technology to
<u>10.</u>

everyone and the Apple II soon _____ (begin) turning up in
<u>11.</u>

business offices, schools, and homes everywhere.

Paragraph Pointer: Narrative Paragraphs

A narrative paragraph tells a story about something that happened in the past. When you write a narrative paragraph, use time order to organize your sentences.

Read the following paragraph *My Trip to Chicago.* The story does not make sense because the sentences are not in the right order. Rewrite the story so that the sentences are in the right order.

My Trip to Chicago

My friend called an ambulance, and it took me to the hospital. On the first day I was there, I fell down on an icy sidewalk and broke my ankle. For the rest of my trip I had to use crutches to get around. Last week I went to Chicago to visit a friend. I spent a whole day in Chicago General Hospital.

_____

_____

_____

_____

_____

_____

_____

_____

PREWRITING

A. Complete the following sentences.

1. One of the _____ (happiest, saddest, scariest, most embarrassing) memories I have of my childhood happened when I was _____ years old.

2. A very _____ thing happened to me on my first day of _____.

3. One summer my friends and I had a(n) _____ experience.

4. My trip to _____ was very _____.

5. One of the most enjoyable evenings I have ever spent was the time _____ _____.

B. Talk about each situation with a partner. Describe what happened to you in each situation.

C. Choose a situation you would like to write about. Make a list of the events you want to include in your story. Number the events so they are in the correct time order.

_____

_____

_____

_____

_____

_____

_____

WRITING

Write a story based on the situation you chose. Use one of the sentences from Exercise A on page 91 as your topic sentence. Then use your list as a guide to write the supporting sentences. Write your story in the past tense. Make sure that the sentences are in the correct time order. Give your story a title.

_____

_____

_____

_____

_____

_____

_____

_____

_____

_____

REVISING

A. Exchange paragraphs with a partner. Read your partner's story and check *yes* or *no* to each question on the Paragraph Checklist. Then help your partner improve his/her paragraph.

Paragraph Checklist		
	YES	**NO**
1. Is there a topic sentence?	❑	❑
2. Are the sentences in the correct time order?	❑	❑
3. Are the past tense verbs in the correct form?	❑	❑

B. Use your partner's suggestions to revise your paragraph. Copy your story onto a separate piece of paper. Share it with your classmates and put it in your portfolio.

Use Your Imagination

A. Look at the photo of a traffic jam. Talk about the photo with a partner.

B. Write a story based on this photo of a traffic jam. Imagine that you are in one of the cars. Tell your reader the time and place of your story in the first sentence. Tell what happened in the next few sentences. Use the past tense.

_____

_____

_____

_____

_____

_____

_____

C. Exchange paragraphs with another student. Read your partner's story. Put your story in your portfolio with the title "A Traffic Jam."

Writing a Biography

PREWRITING

A. Look at the timeline of important events in the life of aviator Amelia Earhart, one of North America's greatest heroines.

B. Write at least one complete sentence for each fact on the timeline.

1. <u>Amelia Earhart was born in 1897 in Atchison, Kansas.</u>
2. _____
3. _____
4. _____
5. _____
6. _____
7. _____

1897	1922	1929	1931	1932	1935	1937
Was born in Atchison, Kansas	Received her pilot's license	Helped found the "Ninety-Nines," an international organization of women pilots that still exists	Married publisher George Putnam, who helped Amelia in her job as a pilot	Became the first woman to fly across the Atlantic alone; received honors from French and American governments	Flew alone from Hawaii to California	Tried to fly around the world but mysteriously disappeared over the Pacific Ocean

USING TIME EXPRESSIONS

When you write sentences about events on a timeline try to use a variety of time expressions. Look at the examples below.

1. **In 1931** Amelia Earhart married the publisher George Putnam. 2. **The next year** she became the first woman to fly across the Atlantic alone and received honors from French and American governments. 3. **A few years later** she flew alone from Hawaii to California.

Look back at the sentences you wrote about Amelia Earhart. Add expressions of time.

WRITING

Use your sentences to complete the paragraph about Amelia Earhart. The topic sentence is given.

Amelia Earhart was a famous aviator.

_____

_____

_____

_____

_____

_____

_____

_____

REVISING

A. Exchange paragraphs with a partner. Read your partner's paragraph and check *yes* or *no* to each question on the Paragraph Checklist. Then help your partner improve his/her paragraph.

Paragraph Checklist		
	YES	**NO**
1. Is there a topic sentence?	❏	❏
2. Are the sentences in correct time order?	❏	❏
3. Are the past tense verbs in the correct form?	❏	❏
4. Are time expressions used?	❏	❏

B. Use your partner's suggestions to revise your paragraph. Copy it onto a separate piece of paper. Share it with your classmates and put it in your portfolio with the title "Amelia Earhart."

PREWRITING

A. Look at the timeline for Seiji Ozawa, a famous Japanese orchestra conductor.

1935	1952	1960	1961–1962	1965–1970	1973–2002
Was born in Hoten, China	Hurt in a rugby accident, turned from piano playing to conducting	Won Koussevitsky Prize for outstanding student conductor	Made assistant conductor under Leonard Bernstein of the New York Philharmonic Orchestra	Served as conductor of the Toronto Symphony	Hired as director of the Boston Symphony Orchestra where he stayed until 2002

B. Write at least one sentence for each fact on the timeline. Use a variety of time expressions.

1. _____

2. _____

3. _____

4. _____

5. _____

6. _____

C. Choose the best topic sentence for a paragraph about Seiji Ozawa. Circle the letter.

a. Seiji Ozawa was hurt in a rugby accident.

b. Seiji Ozawa graduated with top honors from Tokyo's Toho School of Music.

c. Seiji Ozawa is a famous Japanese orchestra conductor.

WRITING

Write a paragraph about Seiji Ozawa. Begin with the topic sentence you chose.

_____

_____

_____

_____

_____

_____

_____

REVISING

A. Exchange paragraphs with a partner. Read your partner's paragraph and check *yes* or *no* to each question on the Paragraph Checklist. Then help your partner improve his/her paragraph.

Paragraph Checklist		
	YES	**NO**
1. Is there a topic sentence?	❏	❏
2. Are the sentences in correct time order?	❏	❏
3. Are the past tense verbs in the correct form?	❏	❏

B. Use your partner's suggestions to revise your paragraph. Copy it onto a separate piece of paper. Give your paragraph the title "Seiji Ozawa" and put it in your portfolio.

A. Look at the timeline for Babe Ruth, a professional baseball player who was the most famous athlete of his time.

1895	1914	1920	1927	1934	1936
Was born in Baltimore, Maryland	Began baseball career as pitcher for the Baltimore Orioles and left to play for Boston Red Sox	Was sold to the New York Yankees	Set a record by hitting 60 home runs in 154 games	Left the Yankees for the Boston Braves	One of the first players elected to National Baseball Hall of Fame

B. Write at least one sentence for each fact on the timeline.

1. _____

2. _____

3. _____

4. _____

5. _____

6. _____

WRITING

Use your sentences to write a paragraph about Babe Ruth. Begin with a topic sentence.

_____

_____

_____

_____

_____

_____

_____

_____

_____

REVISING

A. Exchange paragraphs with a partner. Read your partner's paragraph and check *yes* or *no* to each question on the Paragraph Checklist. Then help your partner improve his/her paragraph.

Paragraph Checklist		
	YES	**NO**
1. Is there a topic sentence?	❑	❑
2. Are the sentences in correct time order?	❑	❑
3. Are the past tense verbs in the correct form?	❑	❑

B. Use your partner's suggestions to revise your paragraph. Copy it onto a separate piece of paper. Give the paragraph the title "Babe Ruth" and put it in your portfolio.

On Your Own

Choose one of the famous people below to write about. Or choose another person and do some research about him or her. Write a paragraph about the person and share it with your classmates.

A. Gabriel García Márquez

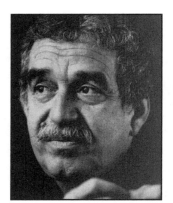

Name:	Gabriel García Márquez
Place of birth:	Aracataca, Colombia
Year of birth:	1928
Occupation:	Author
Accomplishments:	Published his first book of short stories, *Leafstorm and Other Stories* in 1955, wrote the novel *Love in the Time of Cholera* (1985), wrote the non-fiction *News of a Kidnapping* (1996).
Best-known novel:	*One Hundred Years of Solitude*, 1967
Prize:	Won Nobel Prize in literature, 1982

B. Martina Navratilova

Name:	Martina Navratilova
Place of birth:	Prague, Czechoslovakia
Citizenship:	Became a United States citizen in 1981
Birthdate:	October 18, 1956
Occupation:	Professional tennis player
Accomplishments:	National champion in Czechoslovakia from 1972–1975, top-ranked women's tennis player for many years, broke the record of number of titles won in 1992, inducted into the Hall of Fame in 2000.

Writing Your Autobiography

PREWRITING

A. Make a timeline of the important events in your own life.

B. Talk about your timeline with a partner. Ask and answer questions about each other's timeline.

C. Write at least one sentence for each event on your timeline.

1. _____
2. _____
3. _____
4. _____
5. _____
6. _____

WRITING

Use your sentences to write a paragraph about yourself. Tell where and when you were born in the topic sentence. Use the past tense.

_____

_____

_____

_____

_____

_____

REVISING

A. Exchange paragraphs with a partner. Read your partner's paragraph and check *yes* or *no* to each question on the Paragraph Checklist. Then help your partner improve his/her paragraph.

Paragraph Checklist		
	YES	**NO**
1. Is there a topic sentence?	❏	❏
2. Are the sentences in correct time order?	❏	❏
3. Are the past tense verbs in the correct form?	❏	❏

B. Use your partner's suggestions to revise your paragraph. Copy your paragraph onto a separate piece of paper and put it in your portfolio with the title "My Autobiography."

Use Your Imagination

USING POETRY TO WRITE ABOUT MEMORIES

Sometimes it is fun to write a poem about a special memory. Here are some examples of simple memory poems:

Lorentza in Monterrey
4 years old
Sitting in a tree
Waiting for my father to come home from work

Koichi in Tokyo
11 years old
Playing baseball after school
Eating junk food before dinner

Letizia in Forte dei Marmi
17 years old
Playing the guitar
Singing with my friends

Abdullah in Jeddah
8 years old
Riding a donkey
Getting water for my family

A. To write this type of memory poem, think back to a specific time in your childhood. Think about how old you were, where you were, and what you were doing. Use the samples as a guide.

1. On the first line, write your first name and the name of the place where you were. _____

2. On the next line, write your age at that time. _____

3. On the third line, write exactly what you were doing (use the *ing* form of the verb). _____

4. On the last line, give further information about what was going on (use the *ing* form of the verb). _____

5. Make any changes that you want to make in your memory poem. Then copy it below.

_____

_____

_____

_____

B. Write another memory poem.

_____

_____

_____

_____

C. Choose one of your memory poems and read it to your class.

D. Copy your memory poem onto a separate piece of paper and put it in your portfolio with the title "My Memory Poem."

MEMORY DRAWING

A. Think of a special memory from your childhood. Do a very simple drawing of that memory on a separate piece of paper.

B. Use the ideas in your drawing to write a paragraph about this memory. Copy your paragraph under your drawing. When you are finished, put the drawing and the paragraph in your portfolio with the title "A Memory from My Childhood."

◢ Be the Editor

Read the paragraph *An Angry Roommate*. It has six mistakes in past tense verbs. With a partner, find the mistakes and correct them.

An Angry Roommate

I remember the time last year when my roommate, Ellen, gets very mad at me. It was cold that morning, and I borrow a sweater from her. By lunchtime it was warmer, so I taked the sweater off. I forget about the sweater and leaved it in the cafeteria. When I go back to get it, it was gone! My roommate was furious with me. The sweater was a gift from her old boyfriend. His mother had knit it for her. Ellen was so angry and upset that she didn't speak to me for a week.

Real Life Writing

LOST-AND-FOUND MESSAGES

A. Read the Lost-and-Found messages below.

Lost and Found

Lost
Our brown and white Beagle dog—lost near the park. His name is Freckles. My children are heartbroken. If you see him, please call 555-2421.

Lost
Wedding band lost on Peterson Street. I have had it for 30 years, and it is very important to me. If you find it, please call Gabriela at 555-5891.

Found
I found a beautiful, handknit, red scarf in the cafeteria. E-mail me at DB@school.org if you think it is yours.

B. Write your own Lost or Found message.

ADVERTISEMENTS

A. Read about the services offered in the ads below.

Do you need an experienced babysitter? I LOVE KIDS!
References available
Call Samantha at 555-7462

Word Processing
Excellent typing skills, fast,
$5.00 Per Page.
E-mail me at wp@pager.com.

Does Your House Need Painting?
I am experienced and neat.
Reasonable rates.
Call Don 555-4691

Housecleaner Available
Full-time or Part-time,
Honest, Dependable.
Call me at 555-3647

B. Write your own service advertisement.

CHAPTER 9

Writing Your Opinion

Getting Ready to Write

WRITING WHAT YOU THINK ABOUT A TOPIC

A. Look at the pictures below. Match the name of the place or form of transportation to the correct picture. Use the words in the Word Bank. Write the correct word under each picture.

1. _____

2. _____

3. _____

4. _____

5. _____

6. _____

7. _____

8. _____

9. _____

10. _____   11. _____   12. _____

Word Bank

airplane	concert hall	office building	sports facility
airport	hotel room	park	taxi
bus	movie theater	restaurant	train

B. Talk to a partner about where you think smoking should be banned. Draw the "No Smoking" sign on the pictures.

C. Read the paragraphs below and answer the questions that follow.

1.   I think there should be a ban on smoking in public places. First of all, I hate breathing other people's dirty smoke. It is disgusting, but it is also dangerous. People die of terrible diseases from breathing other people's smoke. I also hate it when my clothes smell of cigarette smoke. Another reason smoking should be banned in public places is that it is so bad for the health of smokers. Maybe banning it will help smokers quit smoking. If smokers do not quit because of the cost or the health warnings, maybe these new laws will help them quit.

a. What is the author's opinion?

_____

b. What four reasons does the author give to support his/her opinion?

_____

_____

_____

_____

2.　　　In my opinion, it is unfair to ban smoking in public places. For one thing, why should someone who does not smoke have more rights than someone who does? Also, if non-smokers don't want to be in a smoke-filled room, they can go somewhere else. In addition, smoking is a legal activity. I do not believe the government should tell people that a legal activity is illegal in some places. Finally, I think banning smoking in places like restaurants is bad for business. Maybe both smokers and non-smokers should try to be a little more understanding

a. What is the author's opinion?

_____

b. What four reasons does the author give to support his/her opinion?

_____

_____

_____

_____

Develop Your Writing Skills

USING *SHOULD*

Use *should* or *shouldn't (should not)* when you are giving or asking for advice or an opinion. Look at the examples of sentences that use *should* to express an opinion.

Examples

The county **should** purchase the land to make a park.

You **shouldn't** get mad so easily.

Should I wear my gray dress?

I think you **should** take the chemistry course.

You **shouldn't** drink alcohol if you're going to drive.

He **should** exercise every day.

She **should** take a nap. She looks very tired.

In Statements	In Questions	In Negative Statements
You **should** hang the painting there.	**Should** I hang the painting here?	You **shouldn't (should not)** hang the painting there.
Reggie **should** try to find a different job.	**Should** Reggie try to find a different job?	Reggie **shouldn't (should not)** try to find a different job.

Study these rules for using *should*:

1. *Should* is always followed by the base form of the verb.

   Example

   Maria **should** signed the lease immediately.   (Wrong)
   Maria **should** sign the lease immediately.   (Right)

2. Do not add *s* to *should* even if you are using the third person singular.

   Example

   My brother **shoulds** work harder.   (Wrong)
   My brother **should** work harder.   (Right)

3. Do not use an infinitive (*to* + base form) after *should*.

   Example

   You **should** to stop smoking.   (Wrong)
   You **should** stop smoking.   (Right)

A. Write sentences giving advice using *should*.

1. John has a toothache.

   He should go to a dentist.

2. Matt is late for work.

   _____

3. Frieda has an English test tomorrow.

   _____

4. Peter has the hiccups.

   _____

5. Jong burned his hand.

   _____

6. Lisa has a cold.

   _____

B. Compare your sentences with a partner's. Did you give the same advice?

USING *BECAUSE*

You can use the word *because* to introduce a reason. *Because* answers the question "Why?"

Examples

Why is Frieda studying?

Frieda is studying *because* she has an English test tomorrow.

Why is John going to the dentist?

John is going to the dentist *because* he has a toothache.

Answer the questions using *because*.

1. Why do you think smoking should (should not) be banned in public places?

   _____

2. Why are you studying English?

   _____

3. Why do you think it is important to exercise?

   _____

4. Why do you enjoy seeing new places?

   _____

5. Why are computers helpful?

   _____

Paragraph Pointer: Stating Your Opinion in a Topic Sentence
The following useful phrases are often used to introduce opinions that serve as topic sentences: I believe (that)   In my opinion,   I think (that)   I feel (that)

Write an opinion topic sentence for the five statements in the previous activity.

Example   In my opinion, smoking should be banned in public places.

1. _____
2. _____
3. _____
4. _____
5. _____

PREWRITING

A. State your opinion by completing the sentences with *should* or *should not*. Then share your opinions with a partner.

1. Smoking _____ be banned in public places.

2. American students _____ have to learn a second language.

3. People _____ use cell phones while they are driving.

4. Scientists _____ use animals for their research.

5. People _____ have to retire when they are 65 years old.

6. Governments _____ make the environment their top priority.

7. Driver's education _____ be taught in public schools.

8. Students _____ have to take physical education courses.

9. The custom of tipping _____ be changed.

10. High school students _____ have to wear uniforms.

Paragraph Pointer: Organizing by Order of Importance

You need to give reasons, examples, or facts to support your opinion. It is helpful to list your reasons in the order of importance. The following phrases are often used to introduce facts, reasons, and examples:

First of all,	Also,	For example,
For one thing,	In addition	Secondly,
One reason that	Another reason	Thirdly,
	Moreover,	Finally,

B. Choose three of the opinions you wrote in the prewriting exercise above and give two or three reasons, examples, or facts to support each one.

A. Opinion: _____

Reason 1

_____

Reason 2

_____

Reason 3

_____

B. Opinion: _____

    Reason 1

    _____

    Reason 2

    _____

    Reason 3

    _____

C. Opinion: _____

    Reason 1

    _____

    Reason 2

    _____

    Reason 3

    _____

WRITING

Choose one of your opinions as the topic for a paragraph. Use the opinion topic sentence you wrote. Then use your reasons to write supporting sentences. Remember to use signal words.

_____

_____

_____

_____

_____

_____

_____

_____

_____

_____

REVISING

A. Exchange paragraphs with a partner. Read your partner's paragraph and check *yes* or *no* to each question on the Paragraph Checklist. Then help your partner improve his/her paragraph.

Paragraph Checklist		
	YES	**NO**
1. Does the topic sentence state the author's opinion?	❏	❏
2. Are there at least three sentences to support the opinion?	❏	❏
3. Are the sentences organized according to order of importance?	❏	❏
4. Does the paragraph include signal words?	❏	❏

B. Use your partner's suggestions to revise your paragraph. Copy your paragraph onto a separate piece of paper and put it in your portfolio with the title "My Opinion."

PREWRITING

A. Work with a group of three or four students. Make a list of five things people should do to learn English. Write your ideas on the chart. Write complete sentences using *should*.

Ways to Learn English
1.
2.
3.
4.
5.

B. Compare your chart with another group's. Did you have any of the same ideas? Which ones were the same?

WRITING

Complete the paragraph about the best ways to learn English. The topic sentence is given. Use some of the ideas from your chart for the supporting sentences. End your paragraph with a concluding sentence.

I believe that there are several ways to learn English. _____

_____

_____

_____

_____

_____

REVISING

A. Exchange paragraphs with a partner. Read your partner's paragraph and check *yes* or *no* to each question on the Paragraph Checklist. Then help your partner improve his/her paragraph.

Paragraph Checklist		
	YES	**NO**
1. Does the topic sentence state the author's opinion?	❑	❑
2. Are there at least three sentences to support the opinion?	❑	❑
3. Is there a concluding paragraph?	❑	❑
4. Are the sentences organized according to order of importance?	❑	❑
5. Does the paragraph include signal words?	❑	❑

B. Use your partner's suggestions to revise your paragraph. Copy your paragraph onto a separate piece of paper and put it in your portfolio with the title "Learning English."

PREWRITING

A. Look at the pictures below of inventions and discoveries. Match the name of the invention or discovery to the correct picture. Use the words in the Word Bank. Write the correct word under each picture.

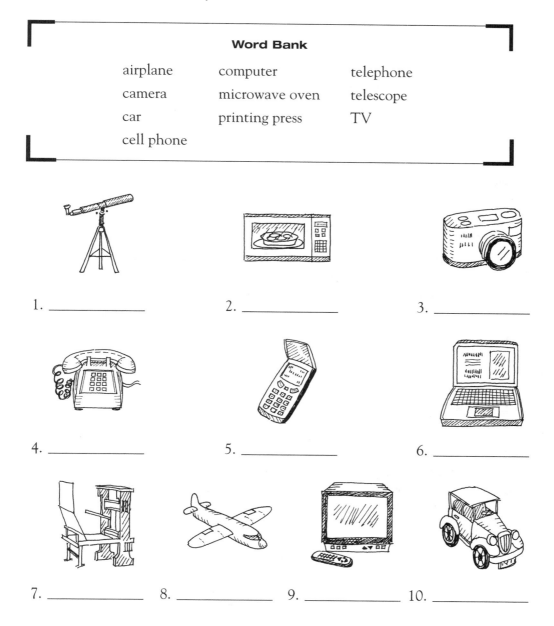

Word Bank

airplane   computer   telephone

camera   microwave oven   telescope

car   printing press   TV

cell phone

1. _____

2. _____

3. _____

4. _____

5. _____

6. _____

7. _____

8. _____

9. _____

10. _____

B. Work with a partner. Ask and answer these questions.

1. Which invention do you think had the biggest impact on society? Why? What specific reasons can you think of?

2. Which invention do you think has had the least impact on society? Why? What specific reasons can you think of?

WRITING

Write a paragraph about the invention you think has had the biggest impact on society. Support your opinion with at least three reasons.

_____

_____

_____

_____

_____

_____

REVISING

A. Exchange paragraphs with a partner. Read your partner's paragraph and check *yes* or *no* to each question on the Paragraph Checklist. Then help your partner improve his/her paragraph.

Paragraph Checklist		
	YES	**NO**
1. Does the topic sentence state the author's opinion?	❏	❏
2. Are there at least three sentences to support the opinion?	❏	❏
3. Are the sentences organized according to order of importance?	❏	❏
4. Does the paragraph include signal words?	❏	❏

B. Use your partner's suggestions to revise your paragraph. Copy your paragraph onto a separate piece of paper and put it in your portfolio with the title "The Most Important Invention."

Use Your Imagination

GIVING ADVICE

A. Read the letter to the Advisor and the Advisor's response. Discuss the situation and the response with a partner.

Dear Advisor

Dear Advisor:

    I met a wonderful man named Joel six months ago. We fell in love immediately, and we have been dating for about six months now. The problem is that he is still dating other women. I want him to stop seeing other women and date only me. Sometimes I have trouble expressing myself when I am talking to people. I think maybe I should send him an e-mail asking him to stop seeing other women. That way, we wouldn't have to see each other's faces. What do you think I should do?

Thank you,
Can't Express Myself

Dear Can't Express Myself:

    I think you can and you should talk to Joel face to face. You should not send him an e-mail on such an important subject. A good relationship is based on open communication. You should talk to Joel, forget him, or wait and see how your relationship develops. It is a bad idea to send him an e-mail instead of talking to him directly. Good luck!

Sincerely,
The Advisor

B. Write your own letter to the Advisor.

Dear Advisor:

_____

_____

_____

_____

_____

_____

_____

C. Exchange letters with a partner. Write a response to your partner's letter.

Dear _____ :

_____

_____

_____

_____

_____

_____

Sincerely,
The Advisor

D. Read and discuss the responses you and your partner wrote to each other's letters.

On Your Own

Write a paragraph giving your opinion on one of the following topics:

1. Hotels should/should not allow pets.

2. People should be able to get a driver's license at age 14/15/16/21.

You Be the Editor

The paragraph has five mistakes in the use of *should*. With a partner, find the five mistakes and correct them.

How to Conserve Water

I think more people should to try to conserve water in their everyday lives. We each use 60 gallons (246 liters) of water every day inside our homes! Conserving water is very important to the future of our planet, and it is also a great way to save money and prevent water pollution. There are several things we should can start now to do every day. One thing is to take shorter showers. A shower shoulds only last about four minutes. Another thing is to turn off the water while we soap our hands, brush our teeth, or shave. In addition, we should used the dishwasher only when it is full. This is true for laundry, too. One of the most important things we should to do is fix leaks immediately. Even a small leak wastes a huge amount of water every hour. These ideas are simple and easy, but they can save a lot of money and they can help save our planet for our kids and grandkids.

Real Life Writing

WRITING A LETTER TO THE EDITOR

A. Read the editorial in today's newspaper about teaching art to children.

> Last week the Board of Education voted to cut art classes from our schools. The Board obviously doesn't understand the importance of art. The Board is right in saying that math, science, history, etc. are important for kids to learn. They are also right in saying that sports are important for kids' health. The Board is wrong, however, to ignore kids' creative side. People need art. Art helps us express ourselves.
>
> Before the members of the School Board make a decision about the education of children, they should educate themselves about the importance of art in our lives. The purpose of our schools is to educate. Is a child educated if he or she is not taught how to make a picture? The purpose of education is to help children become well-rounded adults. Art is a subject worth studying.

B. Write a letter to the editor expressing your opinion about teaching art in school. Do you agree with the editorial?

LETTERS TO THE EDITOR

Dear Editor:

_____

_____

_____

_____

_____

_____

Yours truly,
A Reader

Appendix 1

ALPHABET AND PENMANSHIP

Lower and Upper Case Printed Letters

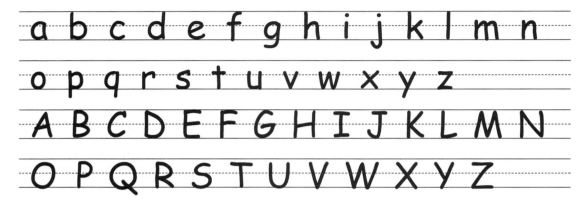

Lower and Upper Case Cursive Letters

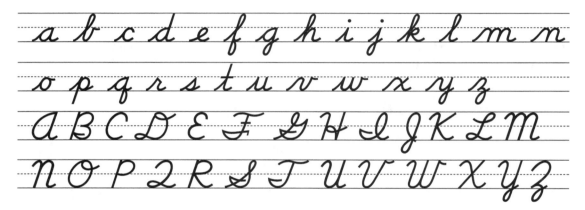

Appendix 2

PAST TENSE FORM OF COMMON IRREGULAR VERBS

Most English verbs are regular. Regular verbs add *ed* to form the past tense. English also has many irregular verbs. Following is a list of common irregular verbs.

become/became	give/gave	see/saw
begin/began	go/went	sell/sold
bring/brought	have/had	sleep/slept
build/built	hear/heard	speak/spoke
buy/bought	hit/hit	spend/spent
come/came	know/knew	take/took
do/did	leave/left	teach/taught
drive/drove	make/made	tell/told
eat/ate	meet/met	think/thought
fall/fell	put/put	understand/understood
feel/felt	raise/rose	wake/woke
find/found	run/ran	win/won
fly/flew	say/said	write/wrote
get/got		

Appendix 3

PUNCTUATION RULES

Punctuation is used to organize written words and guide the reader.

Apostrophes

- Use an apostrophe to show possession.
  My car broke down, so I borrowed Jason's.

- Use an apostrophe to write contractions.
  Yuki isn't going to class today.
  Wally can't find his calculator.
  Why weren't you at the game Saturday?

Commas

- Use a comma to separate three or more words in a list.
  Maria bought apples, oranges, and blueberries at the store.

- Use a comma to separate the day and year in a date.
  They got married on June 29, 2003.

- Use a comma after the name when you write a letter to a friend.
  Dear Henri,

- Use a comma between the name of a city and a state.
  They live in Austin, Texas.

- Use a comma after the words *yes* and *no* in a sentence.
  Yes, I got your message.

- Use a comma when you use *and, but,* or *so* to connect two sentences.
  We will visit my grandmother, and we will also see my aunt.
  Keiko went to the library, but it was closed.
  I lost my book, so I didn't do my homework.

- Use a comma when you **start** a sentence with the words *after, although, because, before, if, since, when,* or *while.*
  Because it was raining, she took an umbrella.
  If he is late again, I will be very angry.
  Since she studies all the time, she is a good student.

- Do **not** use a comma when the words *after, although, because, before, if, since, when,* or *while* are in the **middle** of a sentence.
  She took an umbrella although it wasn't raining.
  We waited outside while he talked to the doctor.
  I had something to eat before I went to the movie.

Answer Key

Chapter 1
You Be the Editor, p. 9

My name is Stanley Ⓢtoico. I am 90 years old. I am from Ⓘtaly. I moved to San Diego, Ⓒalifornia with my family when I was nine years old. I speak Ⓘtalian and Ⓔnglish. Ⓞn my younger years, I had many different jobs. I worked hard and saved my money. In 1955, I started my own business. Ⓣhe business was successful, and Ⓘ retired in 1983. I like to travel and play golf. I have seen and done a lot in my long life. I am a lucky and happy man.

Chapter 2
You Be the Editor, p. 22

My cousin's name is Bettina Lee. She is 37 years old. She was born in
Chicago, Illinois, but now ~~her~~ *she* lives in Denver, Colorado. She is married and
has two children. Bettina and ~~me~~ enjoy spending time together. ~~Us~~ *We* love to go
ice-skating. Bettina is an excellent ice-skater. She skated in ice shows when
~~he~~ *she* was young. Now Bettina teaches ice-skating to young children. She enjoys
watching ~~their~~ *them*.

Chapter 3
You Be the Editor, p. 35

My sister Stephanie is always busy after school. As soon as she get*s* home,
she ~~turnes~~ *turns* on the TV. At the same time, she talk*s* on the phone to make plans
with her best friend. After she ~~watchs~~ *watches* TV and eats a snack, she ~~playies~~ *plays*
computer games or IMs her friends for a while. Then she ~~gos~~ *goes* shopping with
her friends. No wonder she's too tired to do her homework after dinner.

Chapter 4

You Be the Editor, p. 47

Dr. Gary Lesneski is an obstetrician. An obstetrician is a doctor who delivers babies. Dr. Lesneski usually gets up ~~on~~ *at* 6:30 ~~at~~ *in* the morning. He goes to his office at 7:00. His workdays are never typical, but they are always busy. He never knows what time a baby will decide to be born. Sometimes babies are born ~~at~~ *in* the afternoon. Sometimes they are born ~~in~~ *at* night. Often he has to go to the hospital in the middle of the night. He rarely sleeps through an entire night without any interruptions. Dr. Lesneski loves his work, but he looks forward to his vacation ~~on~~ *in* August.

Chapter 5

You Be the Editor, p. 59

My brother's birthday is next week, and I want to buy him a ~~news~~ *new* sweater. In a catalog, I saw one that is made in Canada. I think he will like it. It's a striped (blue) sweater. My brother has eyes (blue) so it will look nice on him. The sweater is made of soft wool, so it is ~~warms~~ *warm*. It is a sweater that fits loosely, so it comfortable (is) to wear. He can wear it to work or on the weekends. I'm so happy I had this idea, and I think my brother will be happy, too!

Chapter 6

You Be the Editor, p. 75

Honolulu is a great place to go for a family vacation because there ~~is~~ *are* many things to do and see. First of all, there ~~is~~ *are* beautiful beaches that are perfect for people who like water sports. For example, Waikiki Beach is one of the most famous surfing areas in the world. ~~Surfing can be dangerous.~~ The hikers in your family will find lots of challenges. For instance, there ~~are~~ *is* a big volcano called Diamond Head that is right in Honolulu. The view from the top of Diamond Head is spectacular. The shopping is also fabulous. ~~Many stores~~ *There are* ~~many stores there are~~ to choose from. Some members of your family might enjoy going to a hula show or a luau dinner in the evening. ~~It~~ *There* is also an aquarium you can visit. It's no wonder that Hawaii is one of the most popular vacation destinations in the world.

Chapter 7

You Be the Editor, p. 86

  Driving on wet or slippery roads can be dangerous. If you are like many ~~mens~~ _men_ and ~~womans~~ _women_, you might not know what to do. When your car starts to skid, these tip$_\wedge^s$ may be helpful. First of all, slowly take your right ~~feet~~ _foot_ off the gas pedal. Then, turn the steering wheel slowly and only as much as necessary to keep your car ~~wheeles~~ _wheels_ on the road. Next, if you have to use your brakes, squeeze them firmly, and then take your foot off the pedal. Finally, do not try to stop or turn quickly. Knowing how to drive on slippery roads can save many ~~lifes~~ _lives_.

Chapter 8

You Be the Editor, p. 104

  I remember the time last year when my roommate, Ellen, ~~gets~~ _got_ very mad at me. It was cold that morning, and I ~~borrow~~ _borrowed_ a sweater from her. By lunchtime it was warmer, so I ~~taked~~ _took_ the sweater off. I ~~forget~~ _forgot_ about the sweater and ~~leaved~~ _left_ it in the cafeteria. When I ~~go~~ _went_ back to get it, it was gone! My roommate was furious with me. The sweater was a gift from her old boyfriend. His mother had knit it for her. Ellen was so angry and upset that she didn't speak to me for a week.

Chapter 9

You Be the Editor, p. 118

  I think more people should ~~to~~ try to conserve water in their everyday lives. We each use 60 gallons (246 liters) of water every day inside our homes! Conserving water is very important to the future of our planet, and it is also a great way to save money and prevent water pollution. There are several things we should ~~can~~ start now to do every day. One thing is to take shorter showers. A shower ~~shoulds~~ _should_ only last about four minutes. Another thing is to turn off the water while we soap our hands, brush our teeth, or shave. In addition, we should ~~used~~ _use_ the dishwasher only when it is full. This is true for laundry, too. One of the most important things we should ~~to~~ do is fix leaks immediately. Even a small leak wastes a huge amount of water every hour. These ideas are simple and easy, but they can save a lot of money and they can help save our planet for our kids and grandkids.